The Little Black Schoolbook

THE SECRET TO GETTING STRAIGHT 'As' AT SCHOOL AND UNIVERSITY

VOLUME 1: ESSAYS

Published in 2008 by Connor Court Publishing Pty Ltd

Copyright (c) Mark Lopez 2008

All rights reserved

Connor Court Publishing Pty Ltd
PO Box 7257
Redland Bay QLD 4165

sales@connorcourt.com
www.connorcourtpublishing.com.au

ISBN: 978-1-921421-07-5

Printed in Australia by Openbook Print, South Australia

Cover design: Cath Pirret Design

For Elaine Lopez

Contents

CHAPTER 1
FIRST PRINCIPLES.. 1

CHAPTER 2
LEARNING THE METHOD: YOUR FIRST STEPS TOWARDS YOUR EMPOWERMENT....13

The three purposes for note-taking:
1. To establish the appropriate persona..............................13
The keen, diligent, capable student..13
The 'chip off the old block'..17

The three purposes for note-taking:
2. To record information about the topic..........................19
The analogy of the 'black shoe'..20
The simile of the cave..22

The three purposes for note-taking:
3. To establish a psychological profile of your examiner........24
Ideology..28
Values...34
Ethics..36
Interests..38
Preferred forms of language...40
Character..42
The fact/value dichotomy...43
Persona...46

The Method in action..49

CHAPTER 3
SUCCESS THROUGH THE MASTERY OF BASIC, ADVANCED AND SUPER-ADVANCED STUDY SKILLS..................55

Getting started: The art of planning, preparation and marshalling resources..................56
Course selection..................56
Subject selection..................57
Selecting your educators..................59
Planning your approach..................60
Organising your resources..................61
General knowledge..................67
Stationery supplies..................68
Helpful allies..................69
Budgeting..................73
Effective excuse letters..................74
Making an unfamiliar environment familiar..................77

Becoming knowledgeable: The art of learning through reading and note-taking..................78
Preliminary or preparatory reading..................79
Determining the most useful texts..................80
The benefits of an early start..................84
Note-taking in class or lectures..................85

Becoming effective: The art of reading and note-taking for research..................90
Selecting topics for study..................90
Understanding the three types of essay questions..................92
Research..................101
Exploratory reading..................102
Selecting the most useful sources..................104
Closer reading of the principal sources..................110
Note-taking for research..................112
Note-taking for shorter essays..................116

Organising study notes for exams...117
More advanced modes of research..118
Dealing with difficult texts..120
Researching without a reading guide...122

Becoming accomplished: The art of essay writing...........124
Understanding the structure of essays..124
The introduction of an essay...128
The bibliography of an essay..131
Citations or footnotes..132
Making a logical argument..132
The formula for masterful essay writing..135

Becoming more accomplished: Additional insights into the art of essay writing...137
Scrutinising the question..137
Brainstorming..138
Structure, planning and execution...139
Organising the footnotes and bibliography..142
Editing...145
Essay archetypes: The analytical narrative and the theoretical review....149
Style: Using scholarly English...151
Style: From competence to mastery..152
Harnessing the power of language..154
Harnessing the power of structure..157

Becoming even more accomplished: The art of creative writing, the analysis of literature, poetry analysis, literature reviews, research reports, essays for vocational courses, problem-solving exercises, public speaking, and course or job applications...162
Creative writing...162
Literary analysis..167
Poetry analysis..171
Literature reviews..173
Research reports..174

Essays for (non-academic) vocational courses..176
Problem-solving exercises..176
Public speaking: From competence to mastery...177
Course applications and interviews...188
Job applications and interviews...191

CHAPTER 4
CLOSING THOUGHTS...193

CHAPTER 1

FIRST PRINCIPLES

Have you ever worked incredibly hard on an assignment by going to great lengths to find impressive alternative sources, then carefully drafted the essay to be just right? Then you handed it in to your teacher in expectation of well-deserved praise, only to be surprisingly disappointed by the result. You then looked at the graded essay and you found your teacher's written comments baffling. This book tells you why you did not receive the expected high grades and what you can do to ensure that you are consistently rewarded with success in the future.

Like you, I had been in precisely that predicament, but instead of just complaining, I started thinking carefully about the problem and what eventually emerged was a powerful new approach to achieving success in education that will help you. While I was a postgraduate student, I worked as a private tutor to make ends meet. While doing so I found that my students faced the same problems that I had, and these methods I had developed also worked for them. I taught these methods to my students, and while doing so I tested and refined them, adding new techniques as problems presented themselves and were solved. Consequently, everything in this revolutionary new approach emerged from *real* experiences solving the *real* problems that *real* students face.

Other study guides tell you how to study but not how to get results. They assume that improvements in conventional 'study skills' automatically equate with improvements in grades, that all educators are competent, that merit is consistently rewarded, and that grading is a scrupulous and objective process. Experience tells us that this is not always the case yet many of us continue in the same old way as if it was. **This is a book about succeeding in *real* education systems in the *real* world**.

It is a book about how you can succeed regardless of whether you have a clever or stupid teacher, a fair or unfair teacher, an objective or biased teacher, a considerate or selfish teacher, an interested or uninterested teacher. This is a book about making both the best and worst dimensions of the education system work for you. It is about how you can succeed no matter what hand you are dealt.

It is easy to sit back and justify poor schooling results by blaming 'the system', a bad teacher or a bad school. The chances are that these unfortunate people are usually right, a bad teacher or a bad school often did contribute to their shortfalls, but it did not have to be that way. It is possible to succeed regardless of the quality of your educators. You will learn that in certain situations it is actually easier to consistently achieve high results with mediocre educators rather than competent ones. **This is a book for those who do not want excuses but want results**.

This book will teach you fundamental study skills, such as how to effectively research and write an essay. It will enable you to achieve what many people desire – merit. Merit can be an important contributor to success but there is more involved in achieving success than merit. **Success in the education system primarily depends on how effectively you deal with people in authority over you.** In this context, displays of merit can be understood as one of the means by which you deal effectively with these people. In addition, it is important to acknowledge that an essay is, in a sense, really an exercise in persuasion. **Every time you submit an essay, you are attempting to persuade your examiner to award you an 'A'.** This book not only covers the basic skills that contribute to the acquisition of merit. It also provides you with the additional means needed to comprehend and control the situations in which you will find yourself. When you are in control of these situations, then you can win consistently.

The teacher and student relationship is analogous to two people on a see-saw. Traditionally the teacher, at one end, is higher and looking down at the student who is at the bottom looking upwards, feeling subordinated, vulnerable and perpetually anxious about what may happen to him. This book guides you towards achieving the power to tip the balance in your favour so you are elevated and confidently looking down at your teacher. Instead of being fearful about how you are assessed, you will know what to say in your essays to make the teacher respond in the way you want.

This book can give you the power to take control over your life and shape your destiny while you are involved with the education system.

Using this book involves taking a major conceptual leap, what is known as a paradigm shift. A paradigm is a framework of understanding and you will need to shift your paradigm in terms of how you understand the education system and how you will succeed in it to get from it everything you want. Although this is a new way of thinking, you will find that it is remarkably close to what you suspected was the real situation all along. In a sense, this new paradigm will free you by showing you how to profit from many of your observations and understandings about how you are being educated.

The first thing you must do is take responsibility for your own education. This means that you must take responsibility for ensuring your success. This first step is challenging, but ultimately it is liberating and empowering. It means that you do not settle for whatever fate deals you. If your lecturer is accomplished and competent, that is good. But if he is not then you need to read more to compensate, borrow the notes of a clever friend or hire an expert private tutor. If your textbook is too complex, poorly written, or boring, then you need to go to the library or book shop and find an alternative to compensate for the other's limitations. If you become dependent on one source of learning you can become captured by it, and therefore vulnerable to becoming a victim of its limitations. If you take responsibility for your own education you can reap the benefits of the wisdom you can acquire from a knowledgeable teacher, lecturer or textbook, while having the ability to compensate for their limitations where necessary. Unless you take responsibility for your education you may find yourself buffeted around by fate.

One of the most rewarding educational experiences is to have complex material explained to you by an insightful expert. I hope that you have many of these enriching experiences as you progress in your studies. Nevertheless, it remains an essential ingredient of your educational success that you do not hand over the control of your learning to others, no matter how good some of them may be. **You must act as if you are your best teacher.** The buck stops with you, not your teacher. You must adopt the attitude that an important, if not the most important, part of learning is what you teach yourself.

You have to succeed in an unfair world. The education system, like many systems, can be unfair. But it can also be rewarding and provide you with what you want from it if you learn how to understand it in order to obtain from it everything it can give you. What this book does is enable you to understand the realties about the education system. **These realities affect the progress of you and every other student regardless of whether you acknowledge them or not.** If you learn to understand these realities, and the study techniques based on them, you can achieve a competitive advantage, the edge needed to succeed consistently. With these methods, it is possible to achieve 'As' with delightful regularity. You will come to expect them. On the occasions when you do not receive them, you will be able to use these techniques to determine why, and what you need to do differently next time. Instead of the examiner having all the cards, these techniques put you in control. **This book is not simply about learning, it is about learning the ropes. It is about being streetwise. It is about playing to win.**

The techniques in this book are easy to comprehend but they are not a quick fix or short cut. There are no short cuts. But by using this book you will avoid the wrong turns and dead-ends that waste time or undermine the achievement of your objectives. These techniques are not easy but they are not difficult either. What they are is effective, consistently effective. For many of you, the change you will make to your life as a result of reading this book will be exciting. With these methods, you can achieve what you want from the education system when you want it, and retain this power for the rest of your life.

To succeed you have to recognise that your educators are human beings, possessing a combination of psychological strengths and failings. Whether you can capitalise on their strengths and avoid becoming a victim of their failings will largely depend on your recognition and exploitation of the psychological dimension of the teacher and student relationship as well as the cognitive process by which your work is graded. Whomever your examiner is does not matter when objective empirical facts are in question. The assessment of whether 1+1=2 or the date of the last federal election will not change whomever your examiners are, provided they are competent. These questions could be assessed by a computer. But many short-answer questions and most essays are different. The essays that are encountered as assignments or in exams, which constitute the core of assessment in the Arts or Humanities, as well as being important in many other subjects, are assessed subjectively.

Although many students wish it was otherwise a grade on an essay represents a subjective opinion rather than an objective fact. It is only the opinion of a particular teacher on a particular day. A grade can often tell you more about what a teacher is like than what an essay is like. Assessments of the same paper by different teachers can vary by 20 per cent or more and still be 'legitimate' or justifiable according the 'professional' opinion of each teacher.

To appreciate the subjective nature of assessment, it helps to compare it to a film review. Have you ever read several reviews of the same film? You may have noticed that for one critic the film was brilliant but to another it was a waste of money. Some reviewers are renowned for preferring action films to romances while with other reviewers it is the other way around. Some reviewers revel in the artistic sensibilities of European cinema while others celebrate the commercial characteristics of Hollywood productions. It follows that if you are sufficiently familiar with the tastes of the reviewers that you could probably predict their reactions to a particular film before they have seen it. You would probably recognise that a reviewer who prefers romances and European cinema will probably not appreciate the latest Hollywood action film no matter how accomplished it was in its cinematic artistry. When critics review films they bring to the process their beliefs, values, tastes and ideological perspectives. This tendency can be readily understood by the following term – bias. Teachers are no different.

A teacher is unlikely to give an 'A' grade to an essay that espouses ideas that they would not vote for in an election. This will be the case no matter how good the essay, although there are examiners who are exceptions their existence does not compromise the usefulness of this rule. My reference here to electoral politics is intended to highlight the role of political ideology in the examination of essays in the Arts and Humanities especially. You can probably recall being told the following by a teacher: 'It does not matter what you say as long as you argue well'. This is rarely the case and if you follow that advice it is at your peril. The teachers who say this probably do not intend to deliberately mislead you.

They may have simply never acquired the ability to distinguish between objective facts and subjective values.

Consequently it pays if you adhere to the following dictum: **Do not follow teachers' advice according to what they say about their attitude to assessment, rather observe their behaviour and learn what to do from what they actually respond to.** People can say almost anything, deceiving others and even themselves, so it is usually their actions that are revealing as to what their true underlying feelings are. Often they will say one thing, such as proclaim their fairness, but act another way, by rewarding all the essays that reflect their biases and penalising those essays that do not.

Never forget that the audience you are actually writing for is your teacher or examiner. Your essay has to appeal to the person who will grade your work. In many English essays, students are asked to specify in a preamble their target audience. In doing this, many students fall into a trap; for example by stating that their target audience was teenage males, believing that this gave them the liberty to write the slang and sexist comments that appeal to this particular audience, not appreciating that their actual audience was a middle-aged feminist teacher with an acute antagonism towards this form of material. This was the experience of one of my students. He was a typical red-blooded teenage male who decorated his dormitory room with posters of fast cars and bikini-clad women. His English teacher had given his class an assignment to write a creative essay. She had provided the class with copies of what she thought was a good essay. The class was expected to use it as a model. This essay expressed the desire for an ideal politically correct world. Each paragraph began with the phrase 'I like...' and expressed the desire for the abolition of racism or war etc. The student did not appreciate the theme but he was inspired by the format. He decided to write an essay about what teenage boys really like. In his preamble he clearly stated that the target audience was teenage males. His 'I like' essay celebrated the joys of action movies and beautiful women, and it included the following witty reference to young females: 'The less dressed is the best dressed'. My student passed a draft of his essay around his dormitory. His peers rocked with appreciative laughter. It was obviously a hit with his target audience, which was a key official assessment criterion. My student handed in his draft to his teacher for comment. Because it was stylishly written, entertaining and perfectly crafted to appeal to its target audience, he expected praise. Her response was far less. She said that it could offend some examiners. What? She was the only examiner. It was internally assessed class work. What the teacher's response really indicated was that she could not give an 'A' to an essay that contravened her fundamental beliefs. Her conscience would not permit it. It would be like expressing approval of ideas to which she was opposed. She hid her true sentiments behind the notion that the student's essay would offend some other examiners. An essay of this kind could never receive an 'A' from this examiner, no matter how well written. To receive an 'A' from her the student would have to write a different essay, one that reflected the teacher's politically correct Left values.

I advised the student to write another essay for his teacher. Interestingly, he chose to submit the original essay. He was proud of it. He claimed that it was the best thing he had ever written. He knew it was first-rate but he accepted that he would have to bear the cost of a grade that was unfairly lower than he deserved. He was confident that he could make up the grades he needed elsewhere. Besides, he was in year 11, not year 12 where every mark counts towards university entrance. Does this kind of experience sound familiar to you? Here is another.

A student of mine, who was doing year 12, was determined to achieve the highest grades. I was tutoring him in a modern history subject that featured the Russian Revolution. He was keen to score high results in a research essay on Lenin's New Economic Policy, the topic the class had been assigned. To get him started I put him in touch with an expert specialist librarian at a leading university who showed him through the library's substantial holdings on the subject. Brimming with enthusiasm, the student read widely and deeply, taking far more effort than would be expected from a high school student. His formidable effort paid off. His first draft was an intelligent, well-structured, well-documented and well-argued essay that was more like university than high school standard. I was very impressed. He submitted the draft to his teacher for comment. He was astonished by the result – only 'C+'. All his previous essays had received 'As'. What was happening? My student was concerned and bewildered. He had put more effort into this essay than the others combined. I looked at his work again. It was superb, I thought to myself, then I realised that was the problem. Unfortunately, it was beyond the intellectual capacity of his teacher to appreciate. What he had to do was 'dumb it down'. We went back to the notes that my student had taken in class. They revealed that his teacher had a very confused and erroneous understanding of the topic. The teacher, of course, did not realise this. Unfortunately, the teacher was unwilling to entertain any interpretation of the subject matter that differed from his own. I advised my student to omit everything from his draft that significantly differed from the teacher's opinions, while the teacher's own thoughts were imputed into the essay, in some cases in the teacher's exact words, no matter how inane some of these thoughts were. My student retained his clear structure and expression, but not much remained of the impressive content of the first draft. My student was willing to do what was necessary to succeed and he did. He received an 'A+' for the essay. That year he achieved a perfect score for History, 100%, and took out the school's History prize. If he wanted to know what the nature of Lenin's New Economic Policy was really like, he could always consult his first draft.

What can we learn from this student's experience? We could start with the following: **Although improvements in quality generally do bring improvements in grades, contrary to widespread assumptions there are circumstances where improvements in quality can be counter-productive in achieving high grades if the examiner is ignorant, incompetent and narrow-minded.** On these occasions you may have to temper the quality of your work that is submitted for assessment.

There is more we can learn from this example. **With some examiners, the achievement of an 'A' does not necessarily involve submitting what you know to be the right answer, but rather what you believe the examiner thinks is the right answer, even if it is the wrong answer.** If you have ever suspected that you have previously been unfairly penalised for having the right answer, you are probably correct. But now you know what you can do about it. If you suspect that your understanding of the topic is too sophisticated for the teacher to appreciate, then you may have to dumb it down by mimicking the teacher's understanding to receive your 'A'.

While helping students as a private tutor I have observed that these kinds of situations are more common than most people realise. They are invisible to the many students who slavishly follow their teacher's instructions and do not take responsibility for their own education. Consequently, they do not have the additional knowledge to serve as reference points for comparison and consequently they do not realise that their teacher is in error and they have learnt incorrect facts or analysis. These students labour under the false assumption that their educator is more competent than he actually is, even though on occasions they may experience the discomforting feeling that what the teacher is saying does not quite add up.

To some students, this revelation about teacher competence may be shocking and it may not conform to what they perceived was reality. Unfortunately, due to the trust these students placed in the system, this reality was imperceptible. For others, you may find in this revelation a considerable vindication. Some students do not realise that they were taught erroneous material until it is too late, when they are externally examined and they find that their learning of this material produced less than the desired results. Some find this out at university, when what they learnt at school is refuted by an expert lecturer. Others find out years later when their faulty knowledge is tested in a situation of employment, when they find that they have to relearn what they learnt in school.

There is even more to learn from this student's experience and other similar examples. We could also recognise the following principle: **A good scholar is not necessarily a successful student, and knowing the difference is the key.** You need to become both. A command of fundamental study skills, the capacity to reason, plus the unleashing of your intellectual creativity and talent will make you a good scholar. But your ability to engage effectively with those who are in authority over you will make you a good student. **With each essay you write, you have to choose whether your objective is to develop your intellectual creativity or to achieve high grades.** On numerous occasions these are not complementary objectives. If you chose to develop your creativity in ways that are contrary to the ideology and expectations of your examiner, you have to recognise that you may pay a price in grades. The method you will learn in this book will help to give you that choice because, firstly, you will appreciate that there is a choice and potential cost involved. I confess that at school and university I often chose, knowing what was at stake, to develop my intellectual creativity and carry the cost in grades, especially in years that were not crucial to my progress to the next stage of the education system. Those essays that were rewarded least were usually my best.

If you choose to be a good student rather than a good scholar then you must be wary of the potential costs that could result from originality. Virtually all examiners claim that they appreciate and reward originality. This is a misleading claim that can lead to many of the most innovative and capable students being profoundly disappointed. Examiners do reward originality but not all kinds of originality. Examiners generally do not reward original ideas that challenge or undermine their ideology or paradigm or upset their comfort zone. These ideas can make them feel profoundly uneasy, even hostile. Wars are fought over ideologies and paradigms so do not underestimate the lengths people may go to protect them. A harsh grade is the least a teacher could do under these circumstances. The originality that examiners do reward is that which can be classified as 'I wish I had thought of that myself'. These are variations of ideas that fit within the examiner's paradigm while introducing, for example, a novel dimension that complements or enhances the examiner's position or viewpoint. Interestingly, the examiners who penalise the more radical expressions of originality would not recognise themselves as doing so because they would perceive the student's original work as wrong-headed or simply wrong. Furthermore, because they have previously rewarded examples of the second kind of originality they would, quite honestly from their perspective, regard and proclaim themselves to be open-minded and fair. As I said earlier: Do not follow teachers' advice according to what they say about their attitude to assessment, rather observe their behaviour and learn what to do from what they actually respond to. Be cautious about presenting your original ideas unless they are of the kind likely to be appreciated by your examiner. Meanwhile, you should record and preserve your more radically original ideas. They are precious, but recognise that your school or university may not be the appropriate forums in which to present them. **If you observe what examiners consistently reward, you will notice that conformity, or at least the appearance**

of it, is the surest means to high grades. This principle was my first realisation of the reality, my first step towards the new method. It seemed to explain to me so much about my past experiences and promise so much for the future by orienting me towards a new direction forward to higher grades. I was 17 and reflecting on my academic predicament during the summer holidays between years 11 and 12. More realisations followed that summer and I commenced the new academic year with a new perspective, a new strategy and renewed enthusiasm. One of the issues that I learnt to appreciate differently was teacher bias.

Teacher bias is one of the issues most complained about by students. I suggest that you look at the issue in a new way, so instead of it being a problem it becomes an opportunity. **Make your teacher's bias your friend because if you do not it will be a formidable enemy.** Once you recognise the subjectivity of assessment, the role of bias, the possibility of teacher error, and the potential cost of originality, it follows that your campaign for straight 'As' must begin by establishing a psychological profile of your examiner. This will enable you to include in your essay everything that you calculate will press the right psychological buttons of your examiner to pay a dividend in grades. You can tailor your essays to suit the idiosyncrasies of each of your examiners. The more obvious their biases the easier your task will be. Once you can read and exploit teacher bias you will be able to play your examiners like a violin.

Before we begin learning the Method, there is another important principle for you to appreciate: **Make your enemies your friends and your weaknesses your strengths.** You should always be thinking about ways in which you can transform people who may be obstacles to your progress into assets or transform things that you do not know into things that you do know. Later I will show you some powerful methods how to do this. In addition to what I can teach you, you should always be thinking about additional ways to solve your particular problems. Free your mind. Think creatively about any problems you face. Do not settle. Do not take 'no' for an answer. This principle also makes the point that you should not accept any adverse situation regarding your skills as unchangeable. Remember that there was a time when you could not read, but you changed that situation by acquiring the skill you needed. You should have the attitude that any weakness you may currently have is not permanent. Your first step to improvement is the recognition of your ability to improve.

CHAPTER 2

LEARNING THE METHOD: YOUR FIRST STEPS TOWARDS YOUR EMPOWERMENT

It all begins with your note-taking in class. First, you set up a page with the date, topic and the name of the teacher or lecturer listed at the top. When the lesson or lecture starts, you take copious notes. Try to take down everything that is said, even if the educator strays off the topic and talks about a current event or even what they did during the holidays. Write in longhand, or shorthand if you have the skill, most importantly you should write in full sentences. Avoid the current fads for note-taking in extremely abbreviated points, or in the form that involves confusing arrays of arrows or 'maps' scrawled across the page. This only creates confusion because these scribbles are perplexingly difficult to decipher at a later date when you read the notes. Your notes must be instantly understandable for them to be of use. By taking notes in full sentences you will not manage to record everything that was said but you will record a great deal. You will become more proficient with experience. But why are we taking these voluminous notes?

The three purposes for note-taking:
1. To establish the appropriate persona

The keen, diligent, capable student

There are three purposes for your note-taking. **Your first purpose is to establish for yourself the kind of persona, or image, that examiners like to reward – that of the keen, diligent, capable student.** To a teacher or lecturer the sight of an attentive student who is hurriedly taking notes conveys to them that you are serious about your studies. It does more than this. Without opening your mouth, your actions are paying your educators a great compliment. You are conveying to them that you find what they say to be so valuable that you are recording it for later use. Imagine how validated you would feel if you were paid such consideration. While most lecturers take it for granted and expect that students take notes (which is another good reason to take them), a number of lecturers and most teachers are quietly flattered by this. You should recognise that many lecturers and most teachers can become favourably predisposed towards positively assessing those students who make them feel good about themselves or make their workday easier. It also follows that educators can become negatively disposed towards the assessment of students who undermine their sense of professional competence or make their workday more difficult. **There is a great deal that affects your assessment that has nothing directly to do with what is written on the page of a submitted assignment or exam.**

While we are on the topic, there is more that you need to do to establish your student persona than engage in fastidious note-taking. You need to be punctual and well organised, even if your educator is not. In addition, as soon as possible in the academic year, you need to 'humanise' yourself in the eyes of your educator so you are no longer merely a face in the crowd. This can be achieved, for example, with a casual conversation where you reveal to your teacher, who is your examiner, your admirable academic aspirations, which, of course, your teacher can help you to achieve. You should be selective about what you tell them about your life and ambitions. It is on a 'need to know' basis. Do not drop your guard. If a teacher asks you: How was your weekend? Do not complain about homework or brag about wild parties or say anything to imply that schoolwork comes second in your priorities. You do not have to be honest, only believable. Remember, your purpose is to orient them towards caring about your future and seeing you as worthy of academic reward.

You should be aware that most teachers, consciously or unconsciously, play a little game in their minds in regards to their class. At the beginning of the year, they like to predict who will achieve the 'As' and who will not. Remember that because teachers interpret the course, teach the course and also grade the students doing the course, this assessment of student potential can easily become a self-fulfilling prophecy. Teachers, often without being fully conscious that they are doing so, can favour those whom they initially picked as winners in order to boost their belief in themselves as seasoned, astute professionals who can predict who will be the top performers. Therefore, it pays to be picked.

Consequently, I advise you to take the necessary steps to always appear to be knowledgeable in class and to avoid asking simple questions. This involves reading ahead, learning your work in advance, so you can provide informed impressive answers in class when the teacher surprises you with a question, which at some stage the teacher is bound to do. Besides, once you establish a head start on your studies, it is almost as easy to keep ahead as to keep up. Furthermore, it does not serve your keen, diligent, capable student persona to ask simple questions in class. Be warned. How many times have you heard teachers tell the class that you are free to ask any question, no matter how simple, only to find they become extremely impatient with the students who take them literally and frequently ask for clarifications? Sadly, teachers can be quick to classify these students as slow learners who are unworthy of high grades. This will seem to these teachers to be, in their eyes, so obviously the case. Remember, they favour those students who make their workday easier rather than more difficult. It serves your interests to treat the class as a venue to display your prowess rather than to inquire. Asking intelligent questions will not compromise your persona, provided that they are not so clever that it embarrasses the teacher. But if you need to ask simple questions, keep them to a minimum, aware of the fact that they could damage your persona. It is preferable to save these questions until after class, when you could safely ask a clever classmate, parent or private tutor.

In addition, it does not pay to 'muck about' or sit in class with those students who do, if you want to achieve straight 'As'. The mildly irreverent or boisterous students who usually constitute the majority of those who congregate in the back row are often those who are full of exuberance and have the greatest sense of fun. Unfortunately, bypassing some of this fun will be part of the cost you will bear on your road to consistently high grades. Enjoy their friendship, but do so at recess or outside school. You have to appreciate that, sadly, most teachers have forgotten what it is like to be young and they sternly overreact to student misbehaviour. Worse than punishing you, they will negatively classify you and treat you in a manner that could jeopardise the achievement of your objective. Some disruptive students, who are usually but not always boys, do so because they find themselves burning with righteous anger after being dealt an injustice by school authorities. Unfortunately, their rebellion only makes their difficult situation worse. I hope that some of them read this book and find in it more constructive, streetwise ways to redirect their energy.

Your establishment of an appropriate student persona is crucial to your campaign to achieve straight 'As'. This is because the elements of this persona correspond with the conceptualisation or schema most teachers have regarding what constitutes a first-rate student. To them, it just seems appropriate or fits snugly in their imaginations when high grades are awarded to certain people. Meanwhile, the awarding of high grades to those who do not present the appropriate persona will, for some reason they cannot quite explain, feel like a mismatch that can make them uncomfortable at a gut level. Consequently, they may hesitate, holding back from awarding an 'A' to a student with an inappropriate persona whose performance is on the border between a 'B' and an 'A' because it just does not feel right to them. Meanwhile, if you have established the appropriate persona and you have made a small mistake, such as moderately exceeding the word length limit on an essay, your teacher may be reluctant to deduct marks because to do so would contravene their positive conceptualisation of the worthiness of this student.

The value of having established the appropriate student persona was appreciated by one of my year 12 English students. He initially came to me late in year 11, requiring help in fundamental study skills, such as essay writing (these and other skills are explained later in the book). I provided him with a solid foundation in this regard while also teaching him the Method. He did very well in his year 11 final exams, and when he commenced year 12 he quickly established the persona of the keen, diligent, capable student. The advantages of this were soon apparent. My student sensed that his teacher had picked him as one of her top students. His initial essays were of a high standard and he received the 'As' that he deserved. Then something interesting happened. My student's performance slipped as he found himself unintentionally reverting to some of his previous bad essay writing habits that I thought we had effectively addressed. His work dropped below an 'A' standard but interestingly his teacher continued to award him top marks. She had obviously become biased in his favour and my student's clever exploitation of his persona would have contributed to this. My student and I soon fixed his essay writing problem so the standard of his work again matched the high grades that he was awarded. He finished the year triumphantly with 86% for English.

The 'chip off the old block'

Almost all people prefer others who remind them of themselves or at least appear to be like-minded. Consequently, the persona that I recommend as advantageous for you to adopt at university is what I term the 'chip off the old block'. Although this idiomatic phrase literally evokes the notion of 'like father like son', I am using it less precisely to imply that your persona should ideally remind your academics of themselves when they were young. Many lecturers and tutors have a passionate interest in their subjects and an appreciation of scholarly virtues. If you appear to be genuinely interested in this subject, as well as seeking a credit or distinction in the hope of qualifying for an Honours year and ultimately pursuing postgraduate study, they are more likely to look favourably on you than the other nameless students passing through on the way to acquiring that 'piece of paper', the degree. Remember that the keenness you need to demonstrate is not mere wide-eyed enthusiasm, it should be evident to your academics in the hard work that has allowed you to develop a conversant knowledge of the subject ahead of the others in your tutorial, just as these academics did when they were undergraduates.

Another dimension of your 'chip off the old block' persona is your dress and manner. Fortunately, most academics are reasonably comfortable with dress styles that are hip or fashionable, but there is a limit to what they appreciate. I recommend that you do not come to lectures and tutorials looking as if university is something to keep you mildly amused in between nightclubs. Neither should you appear as if you would rather be at the beach and you are waiting for the tutorial to end so you can grab your surfboard and race to the coast. Appear as if you spend a great deal of time reading. Remember, they do. They will recognise the symptoms of excessive reading and it will warm their hearts and make them appreciate you as someone on the road to becoming 'one of us'.

At university, the tutorials are the crucial arenas where you establish your persona because that is where you encounter the academics up close. I remember that when I was at university, I had elected to do Political Sociology as one of my second year Politics subjects and I was looking forward to it. The guest lecturer for that semester was a London-based academic who had written the principal textbook used in the course. In addition, the tutor assigned to assist him was one of the most capable in the Politics Department. To introduce himself, the lecturer joined with the tutor in attending the initial tutorials. Showing the first weary signs of jet lag after his long flight, the lecturer asked each student to state why they had chosen to study Political Sociology. I was astonished at the number of students who responded with banal statements like 'It fitted in with my timetable', oblivious to the disheartening insult they had inadvertently delivered to someone who had traversed continents to be there. I was the last person asked, to which I replied that political sociology provided the conceptual foundation for any study of politics, so as far as I was concerned it was essential. Rather than intending to make a positive impression, I had simply answered honestly. However, I found the noticeably positive reaction of these academics intriguingly instructive. From that moment, my status rose dramatically in the estimation of these academics and I remained the only student in that tutorial whom they treated seriously, or rather, whom they treated as a chip off the old block.

Before we continue to cover the second purpose of note-taking, it is necessary to provide a warning about 'crawling' or sycophancy, which is quite different from what I advocate. What I advise you to do is to establish an effective persona that will help you to control and make the most of your interpersonal encounters in the education system, sometimes through subtle and effective psychological manipulation. Crawling lacks dignity and it can compromise the self-respect that is a significant ingredient for success. Nevertheless, it should be acknowledged that crawling can achieve results. It is amazing how many teachers will respond positively to the crawler's gushy, effusive, 'sucky' displays of attention. Be aware that the people who respond positively to the crawler's flattery are usually those whose egos need boosting from others because they harbour inner doubts about their true ability or merit. That is why you will notice more positive responses to crawling from teachers than academics who are generally more self-assured. Crawling can leave these people cold, even annoyed, and although they may be polite to the crawler's face they would secretly harbour a distaste that would be detrimental to the crawler. These people are impressed by a positive industrious demeanor and a passion or thirst for knowledge, qualities with which they can identify, rather than the shallow attentiveness of the crawler. They expect more substance than simply display. Crawlers may do well with some educators but their weakness is that they are usually a 'one act show'. They are not flexible enough to tune into the range of personalities of examiners or the diversity of situations in which they find themselves so they often appear tactless. Another drawback of crawling is that it alienates most peers who find crawling dishonourable. This can be a disadvantage when trying to establish networks of friends who can provide valuable support and advice.

The three purposes for note-taking:
2. To record information about the topic

Your second purpose for note-taking in class or lectures is to record all the information about the topic (the facts, analyses and explanations) that you will need. Interestingly, this is what most students understand to be the only purpose of note-taking. This material is particularly important if your teacher or lecturer is competent, capable or talented. Seize the opportunity to capture the valuable pearls of wisdom that fall your way. Some of my fondest memories of university are of furiously note-taking while a talented academic delivered a lecture that was a tour de force, bristling with enlightenment. You could almost feel yourself becoming more intelligent with every word they uttered.

Note-taking is even more important if your teacher or lecturer is incompetent or in error. Unfortunately, when this is the case, many students put down their pens in frustration, sometimes while muttering obscenities under their breath, at precisely the time when they should be diligently recording this information. This information is crucial if this teacher or lecturer is your examiner. This is because they will be assessing your work against their concept of what the right answer is, and not against any other potentially right answers. Therefore, to achieve straight 'As', this information is indispensable and you must have it at your disposal. **Despite what most people would ideally like to be the case, you are likely to be rewarded for reflecting your teacher's mistakes and penalised for correcting them. It is vital to your success that your submitted work reflects as closely as possible your examiner's understanding of the topic.** To help you effectively comprehend and achieve this task I have developed what I term the analogy of the 'black shoe'.

The analogy of the 'black shoe'

Most teachers and a number of lecturers have difficulty in entertaining the philosophical possibility that there may be more than one approach or valid answer to a question. When interpreting the requirements of an assignment or task that is listed in the curriculum, most teachers mentally put themselves in the position of someone doing the task, then imagine what they would do to complete it or what they imagine the right answer to be. In their minds they award their approach or answer an 'A+'. Later they use it as a yardstick by which to assess the students' attempts at the same assignment. The black shoe analogy explains this process and the consequences for the students.

Assume that the assignment is the definition of footwear. Your examiner has imagined what he believes the right answer to be and come up with the image of a polished black shoe. Remember that the assignment is footwear, which is quite broad and varied in nature. Suppose one student submits the image of a tin can. The examiner will mentally compare his image of the black shoe with that of the tin can, find that they do not match and mark it accordingly. This student does not succeed. Suppose another student submits the image of a sandal. I remind you that the assignment is the definition of footwear. The examiner compares his image of the black shoe with that of the sandal and finding that it does not match, marks it accordingly. This answer was also unsuccessful in impressing the examiner. Both the sandal and the black shoe are correct answers yet the student submitting the sandal suffered because it was not the answer imagined by the examiner. Of course, in addition to the sandal, there are many other potentially correct answers that would not be recognised. Now you know why there are many essays that deserve an 'A' that are not rewarded because they do not correspond to what the examiner imagined the right answer to be.

The black shoe analogy also helps to explain why an essay may receive an 'A' from one teacher yet if it was taken to the class next door and submitted unchanged to another teacher it may only receive a 'C', or vice versa. It also helps to explain why some students who seek high marks through achieving merit can find themselves surprised by unfair, disappointing results. It also helps to explain why the teachers who profoundly disappointed these students perceive themselves to be professionals who are accurate, fair and just. It may also help to explain why so many famous, creative, brilliant and accomplished people did moderately well or poorly at school.

Many but not all examiners have a narrow subjective concept of what constitutes excellence. However, the exceptions do not compromise the value of this rule: **To succeed with each of your examiners it is essential to identify their 'black shoe'.** The approach that can be derived from the analogy of the black shoe is one of the reasons why the students who use my method can consistently receive the highest grades from any examiner. Before they proceed with a submitted assignment they determine their examiner's black shoe and fashion their answer to suit it. In addition, if they identify whether their examiner can entertain the possibility of more than one correct answer, and if there is greater scope for being rewarded for originality or merit, they respond accordingly.

There is more that you can do to identify your examiner's black shoe than take detailed notes in class. You could perform some detective work to identify the source or sources that your examiner used to learn the subject, then familiarise yourself with them. This was done by one of my year 12 English students. Firstly, he had taken responsibility for his education, initially by consulting me as a private tutor and then by purchasing every available set of published notes on the novel that he was studying. His English teacher, who was the school's English coordinator, was conducting the lesson by reading to the class from notes that were concealed from their view behind his clipboard. While listening attentively and taking copious notes, my student became unnerved by the feeling that the content of this lesson seemed uncannily familiar. That evening, my student checked through the various notes he had purchased to discover that the lesson was derived word for word from one of them. He concluded that his teacher had photocopied this material and attempted to pass it off as his own analysis. My student was initially outraged that his teacher, who is paid a substantial salary, was plagarising a $12 booklet to serve as his lesson. But after we discussed the discovery further, my student realised that this was actually a godsend. He had clearly identified his examiner's 'black shoe', his examiner's understanding of the right answer. My student then successfully exploited his detective work to achieve an 'A' by basing his essay heavily on this material. This student profited from the power of the black shoe analogy. So too, can you.

The simile of the cave

To further your appreciation of the black shoe analogy I would also like to introduce you to some classical Greek philosophy, Plato's simile of the cave, or rather my variation on it. I was introduced to this fascinating philosophical argument while studying first year Philosophy at university and I have benefited from it ever since. Although Plato used the simile of the cave to explain the difference between what he saw as absolute truth and the illusion of truth, and why some people can prefer illusion to reality, I found it helpful in understanding why some teachers can be so inflexible, uncompromising and even hostile when their intellectual comfort zone is challenged by a student.

Plato asked his readers to imagine a large cave, where everyone living in it had their heads and bodies fastened so they could only look straight ahead and all in the same direction. Behind them is a powerful source of light, a great fire. In front of this fire, between it and the backs of the inhabitants, are objects drawn from the real world that cast shadows on the cave wall in front of the inhabitants. These shadows were all that these people could see. Only able to see shadows, these people would assume that they were what constituted real objects or reality. To these people, the shadows would represent the truth. Plato argued that if these inhabitants were told that the shadows were an illusion they would confidently disagree because they were used to assuming that what they always saw was true. Plato added that if these people were forcibly turned around to look into the light and at the real objects, the glare and surprise would be too painful for them to bear, so most would prefer to turn around again, back towards the world of the shadows, which was comfortable and predictable.

If students, particularly clever ones, say, do or write something that challenges a teacher's concept of reality or their intellectual comfort zone, this can be painful for the teacher. I mean this literally. It can cause them psychological distress that is painful to experience. Consequently they seek to remove the cause of the distress to restore their equilibrium, and diminishing the apparent worth of a student's opinions by awarding low grades can be one means of achieving this.

The wisdom of Plato's simile of the cave became apparent to one of my year 12 English students. She had approached me initially because her teacher did not understand, so therefore had not taught, an important section of the course, and she required the additional assistance of a private tutor to compensate for this shortfall. This student was very intelligent and a fast learner, and I ensured that she went away with a sound grasp of the knowledge and skills she required. Having addressed her problem I did not expect to hear from her again. I was surprised when she came back. The knowledge and skills with which she had been provided had not produced the desired results. She received a 'B'. I checked her work. It was excellent. I quickly reassured the student of her ability. I wondered whether the problem stemmed from her relationship with her teacher. 'Is your teacher open-minded?' I surreptitiously inquired. 'Oh yes', my student exclaimed. She enthusiastically told me that her teacher was a devout Christian while she was an atheist, and the two of them would engage in vigorous philosophical debates about the existence of God and other theological matters. Oh no, I quietly thought to myself while my student assured me that her teacher did not object to her opinions. Elements of her account suggested to me that the reverse was the case and my student was unaware of this. I suspected that this situation represented a prime demonstration of the fact that there is a great deal that affects a student's assessment that has nothing directly to do with what is written on the page of a submitted assignment or exam.

While some people are relaxed and confident about their beliefs, others are more sensitive and less able to accommodate the well-intentioned but provocative intellectual jousting that can come from a young, precociously intelligent mind trying out its spurs. I advised my student that I suspected that these philosophical discussions were the cause of the low grades even though religion was not relevant to the subject matter of the work that was unfairly assessed. I recommended to my student that she cease these discussions immediately because they were challenging her teacher's intellectual comfort zone. Her teacher was not as broad-minded as my student assumed. She was just skilful at disguising her discomfort. Having identified and stopped the cause of the problem, we also needed to do something to turn the situation around by associating my student with ideas that confirmed and validated the teacher's beliefs. My student's next assignment provided us with the opportunity.

The class had to compile a creative writing portfolio that included a 'personal' essay, which was supposed to be autobiographical. My student wrote an essay about how her brother had a near-death experience and, as a result, converted to Christianity, a belief system that has since brought him much solace. My student wrote about how she respected her brother's beliefs and appreciated the benefits they had brought to his life. My student did have a brother, but he was not a Christian. That was not important. The essay produced the desired result. My student's grades shot up to the 'A' level and stayed there.

The three purposes for note-taking:
3. To establish a psychological profile of your examiner

The problem that my student faced was solved and the story had a happy ending, but this problem could have been avoided altogether had this student initially been aware of the third purpose of note-taking. **The third purpose of note-taking is to gather the information you need to establish a psychological profile of your examiner so that everything you put in your essay can be calculated to pay a dividend in grades.** Many students do not realise that there is a great deal more being communicated in class, other than the facts, analyses and explanations related to the lesson, that will have a profound impact on their success. In addition to, or as a sub-textual dimension of, the content of the lesson the teacher or lecturer may be communicating ideology or values that will have a crucial influence on how you are assessed. When the teacher wanders off the topic to make jokes at the expense of the prime minister or to chat affectionately about family life, most students, who have been diligently taking notes during the lesson, put down their pens and rest. If the teacher is particularly self-indulgent in their monologue, some students find themselves, despite their good intentions, bored and staring out the window. Wrong move. If you do this you too will miss what most students fail to record because they do not see its relevance, the crucial information that will indicate to you how your examiner ticks, what is important to them, what they positively or negatively respond to, and the perspective from which they will perceive you and your work.

In addition to your notes on the content of the lesson, you need to simultaneously make another set of notes by recording the material that will allow you to make a psychological profile of your examiner. Different students have adopted different methods of doing this. When their teacher suddenly reveals relevant information, some of my students change the colour of the pen they are using, or switch to pencil, or write in the margin, or draw a box around this material to distinguish it from the regular notes. Whatever means you use is not important, it is the fact you are gathering this information that matters most.

This note-taking requires astute careful listening and observation. It is a bit like espionage. It is the intelligence gathering that will enable you to precisely plan and execute the effective strategy and tactics to bring victory in each battle of your study campaign. Put another way, you are gathering the information that will give you the decisive persuasive edge in every interpersonal encounter, whether it is an essay or a conversation with your teacher. With this information at your disposal, your examiners will be dancing to your tune, not the other way around. Once you are competent at acquiring and using this information, your days of anxiety while waiting for your results, an anxiety that stems from uncertainty about the behaviour of your examiners, will be replaced by a relaxed confidence that is grounded in an understanding of your examiners' strengths and weaknesses and how to capitalise on them.

You need to recognise that the process of grading essays, especially essays that the examiners like, is not simply a cold, calculated, mechanical process. It is closely associated with particular noticeable feelings or emotions. Examiners feel particular emotional sensations such as delight, pride in the student's performance, personal or professional validation, or they are simply reassuringly impressed by the improvement of the student as they write 'A' on the page of an essay. Therefore, it follows that your ability to influence the emotions that are associated with the awarding of high grades will put you in a position to decisively influence the cognitive process through which you are assessed. **If you can tailor your submitted work to produce the feelings in your examiners that they associate with the awarding of 'As' then you can virtually generate 'As' at will.** Of course, if you are to do this you need to have the necessary psychological information at your disposal. Luckily, it will be all around you, only you have to become skilled at recognising it.

Before I teach you how to gather this valuable information and how to use this powerful method, I need to explain to you more about the relationship between reason and emotion. One of the founding principles upon which liberal-democratic societies are based is that all individuals are rational and the best judges of their own interests. This is arguably a noble and valuable normative principle but what it tells us about human nature is problematic and partially misleading. It is true that humans have the capacity to reason but this ability is controlled by the emotional state they may be in at the time. For example, if people are hungry or jealous, they will process certain information differently than if they were in other emotional states. Once the hunger subsides or the jealousy passes, they usually perceive the same phenomena in a different fashion. At a subconscious level, many people instinctively appreciate the impact of emotion on their reasoning. This is evident when they sense they may be in the wrong emotional state to productively respond to, for example, a business proposition. Their reply, 'I'll sleep on it', means, in part, that this person wants to allow their emotional state to shift to one that is more conducive to a clear evaluation of the pros and cons. You may also have recognised the impact of emotion on reason when you appreciated that when your parents were angry with you that it was not the time to ask them for money. You waited, choosing a moment when they were proud of you and then you asked. Alternatively, you charmingly reminded them of why they loved you and at the moment when their mood softened, and irrepressible smiles sneaked across their faces, you asked them for the money.

This principle applies to your assessment. To receive an 'A' for your essay, you need to generate in your examiner the emotional state in which they award top grades. Your essay, in particular the opening paragraph, requires the appropriate content to generate this prerequisite condition for effective persuasion. Fortunately, the content that has this magical transformational effect is not difficult to find. It is in their bias. **There are few things more pleasing to examiners than to see their opinions and values reflected back in their students' work.** It has a powerfully positive effect on their emotional state. What happens when you do this is that your examiners will see a little piece of themselves in your work, and what grade are they going to want to award this piece of themselves? You guessed it, an 'A'. But it does more than this. It puts them into what I describe as a 'non-critical frame of mind'. In this emotional state, they will not notice the little errors that can be scattered throughout many students' essays. They will not be looking for them. Consequently, these students will not be penalised for them. On the other hand, if your work counters their opinions and values, your examiner will instantly slip into what I describe as a 'critical frame of mind'. In this state, they will voraciously search for every possible mistake they can find in order to justify their strong feelings that, in their eyes, this student's work is 'below standard'. If you go against your examiner's bias it is a formidable enemy, but if you decide to exploit their bias you can virtually control their response to your submitted work without them having any idea what you are deliberately doing. Moreover, once you have done it the first time, you can do it again and again, with all of your examiners. In fact, they will praise you for what you do. It will be your work that makes them happiest, giving them uplifting feelings of vocational success and validation. This pleasing circumstance is what is celebrated in contemporary management jargon as a win/win situation.

To establish your psychological profiles of your examiners, you gather information under seven categories: ideology, values, ethics, interests, preferred forms of language, character, and persona. I shall discuss each of them in turn.

Ideology

Ideology refers to a comprehensive and systematic set of ideas, concepts, beliefs and values about the nature of the world, mankind, society, the ideal form of society and how to achieve it. You can recognise most ideologies as ending in the suffix 'ism', such as socialism, communism, liberalism, conservatism, or nationalism. We all subscribe, in our own ways, to an ideology or an amalgamation of aspects of several ideologies, even though many people are unaware that they do because they do not see themselves in these political terms. Ideology is at the core of our framework for understanding the world. Consequently, if you understand someone's ideology you have taken a significant step towards understanding them.

Some teachers or lecturers are quite open about their beliefs. I have had several lecturers who openly declared in their initial lectures or tutorials that they are Marxist. You will find that most educators are more coy about this subject. Despite this, they leave many clues. Here are some things to listen for and record. They may take strong stands on high profile issues that make it clear that they share the ideologies of particular political parties. They may also make ideologically revealing statements such as: 'There will be no homophobia in this classroom' (gay rights); or 'The reality is that Australia is a multicultural society' (anti-racism/ multiculturalism). Some educators will give clues in their appreciation of certain books or films, such as *To Kill a Mockingbird* (anti-racism), or in their admiration for particular celebrities or political leaders, such as Nelson Mandela (anti-racism again), or by decorating their office door with overtly political cartoons cut from newspapers. If your educator jokes at the expense of a particular politician or public policy this usually suggests that they have a particular underlying ideological perspective that informs and directs these, usually sarcastic, comments. Some clues are even more subtle, being evident in their tone or manner as they discuss particular topics that are potentially ideological. If they are animated, effusive, or smiling while they discuss, for example, bushwalking in 'unspoiled nature', this could indicate approval for environmentalist principles. Meanwhile, if they talk in a monotone, or stand with their hands by their sides, or they hurry through a topic, this often indicates disapproval or opposition or a lack of interest in the topic under discussion. Because ideologies are systematic, the revelation of one key belief usually indicates the existence of other related linked beliefs. For example, a pacifistic anti-American attitude to international relations can betray an educator's allegiance to the whole canon of politically correct Left principles. Once you are skilled at this process of identification and classification, you will need only a few clues to determine with reasonable accuracy your examiners' opinions on most political topics.

For Australian students their task of classification is made easier by the fact that the vast majority of teachers in Australia, my estimation is about 90 per cent, and many academics subscribe to the amalgamation of ideologies that can be classified as the politically correct Left, although significant pockets of economic rationalism can be found in the areas of economics and business studies. Similar situations exist in education systems throughout the Western world. It follows that to understand your educators it is necessary to have a working knowledge of the ideologies that will profoundly influence your education and assessment at this time in history.

The amalgamation of ideologies that we currently understand as the politically correct Left emerged during the 1960s when it was originally referred to as the New Left and the (hippy) counter-culture. These beliefs are comprehensive and elaborate, but for your purposes they can be understood as roughly falling under six major categories that could also be seen as ideologies in their own right: pacifism, anti-racism, Marxism, environmentalism, feminism and gay rights. Protests against the United States and Australia's participation in the Vietnam War, in particular, helped to spread these ideas among the youth of that period, the 'baby boomer' generation, especially those in tertiary education and even more significantly those who studied the Arts and Humanities. During the early 1970s, there was a massive recruitment of young teachers into the school system that included many of these politicised graduates. Their presence dramatically transformed the ideological complexion of this major socialising institution. That is why you would have noticed that about half of the teachers in Australia are about the same age, currently in their fifties, and why they share the same beliefs that are essentially those of their formative years, which have been continually validated and reinforced by their peers. In addition to this, the simultaneous capture of teacher-training institutions and substantial sections of university Arts and Humanities faculties by politically correct Left academics ensured that this ideology was transmitted to the younger generations of teachers who followed, most of whom enthusiastically adopted these ideas as their own.

The term 'politically correct' (along with its synonym 'ideologically sound') achieved currency during the 1980s. It was first used by the politically correct to negatively label as 'politically incorrect' those people with differing opinions, thereby pressuring them to conform. The correctness or soundness of an individual was measured in terms of their conformity to various ideological concepts, values and ethical principles rather than to empirically verifiable facts, which remained a secondary consideration. A backlash against political correctness emerged during the early 1990s, when the term was turned back onto the former accusers, many of whom then distanced themselves from the label politically correct, which had taken on negative connotations. Nevertheless, the label stuck, effectively replacing the terms New Left and counter-culture.

Those who subscribe to the politically correct Left ideology share the following beliefs: a progressive interpretation of history; a favouritism for pressure group politics as quintessentially democratic as well as an affection for street protests as a form of political culture; a preference for government regulation or spending to solve social problems; an attitude that ethics (or social justice) should constitute the basis of politics; a fascination with social divisions along the lines of race, ethnicity, class, gender or sexual preference and support for positive discrimination to address perceived inequalities in these areas; a preoccupation with censoring forms of speech deemed politically incorrect; and an idealistic belief that mankind is not static in nature but improvable, largely through education and re-education. Consequently, they would feel it is their moral duty to transmit their beliefs to the young in order to bring about their concept of the better world.

The impact on the school curriculum of this ideology has been profound. Consequently, you will notice that, for example, virtually every text set for study in a subject like English reflects and promotes politically correct beliefs. Where they may differ from the norm is usually when an otherwise politically correct author showed an appreciation of a politically incorrect belief drawn from, for example, conservative, nationalist, or Catholic thought that is incorporated into an overall politically correct argument. Alternatively, the older classic texts that have been chosen for study have been reinterpreted from a politically correct perspective. They are then taught in a fashion that privileges this interpretation over the original meaning for the original audience. It should be noted that the official curriculum selection criteria for texts does not state that their purpose is for indoctrination, yet the criterion that it be 'worthy of study', when interpreted by a politically correct mind, almost inevitably results in the selection of books, or interpretations of books, that reflect and promote politically correct ideas.

The principal ideological exception to the dominance of political correctness in the Australian education system is economic rationalism. Although it largely represents a revival of classical liberal economics of the eighteenth and nineteenth centuries, it emerged during the late 1970s in Western nations like Australia, in part, as a counter to the New Left or political correctness. It soon found accommodating homes in various Economics faculties and departments. This ideology believes in individualism and the efficiency and effectiveness of the market in the distribution of goods and services. It also conceptualises human wants and needs primarily in economic terms that are satisfied through economic activity. Interestingly, this ideology is also progressive but it sees progress differently to the politically correct. It is pro-business, pro-growth, and supports economic deregulation and free trade as means to greater prosperity. It is sceptical of the role of government spending to solve social problems. It also puts a premium value on individual liberty, preferring to advocate economic self-reliance, low taxes, choice, and to use incentives rather than regulations to influence behaviour. The influence of this ideology on the curriculum has been mainly confined to economics and business subjects, which have enjoyed a revival in recent years. Otherwise, the overwhelmingly dominant ideology influencing educators and curricula is political correctness.

Why is it so important to know this? In addition to allowing you to better understand your class teacher who stands before you several times a week and also assesses your internally or class-assessed assignments, it provides you with the following vital advantage. **Your understanding of ideology enables you to determine with sufficient accuracy the biases of your unseen examiners, those anonymous people drawn**

from the pool of teachers who correct the exams that are assessed externally from your school. Able to determine the biases of your unseen examiners, you can exploit them as readily as those of your class teacher. In preparation for the externally assessed year 12 English exam I drill my students until I am confident that they know the politically correct answer to any question that they may be asked. For example: Question: What side would you take in the debate about the admission of women into combat roles in the military? Answer: You would support their admission on feminist grounds of equal opportunity and recruitment on the basis of merit rather than gender. Question: In a confrontation between developers and an environmental pressure group which side would you take? Answer: You never take the side of big business and always side with the environmental pressure group, or any politically correct Left pressure group, especially one with the word 'rights' in its title. Question: In a dispute between animal rights groups and duck hunters which side would you take? Answer: If you side with the hunters, you are a dead duck. People use ideology, either consciously or unconsciously, to distinguish between those whom they consider to be either 'one of us' or 'one of them'. It follows that is far more advantageous regarding your assessment if your examiner perceives you to be 'one of us'. For those students who share the politically correct beliefs of the examiners on various questions, their task is made a little easier. The others have to become adept at a necessary deceit.

'Playing the game', the study game, allows you to provide your examiners with what they want to hear to get your 'As'. But by adopting the attitude that it is a game allows you to protect your integrity, your precious integrity, so you are free to adopt the beliefs that you choose. You may choose to adopt the beliefs of some of your educators or you may not. That is up to you to decide as you use the education system to become the person who you want to be rather than whom your educators intend you to be.

When students use this method of exploiting the ideological bias of their examiners it dramatically increases their odds for success. One of my students, who began with me late in year 11, commenced year 12 attuned to the Method and full of confident enthusiasm. I shall never forget his excited telephone call to me on the evening of his first day back at school. Barely containing his glee, he told me that his 'A' was 'in the bag'. He recounted how his teacher had proudly told her class that she had written a letter to the teachers' union explaining that it would save paper and be better for the environment if they distributed their union bulletins by email rather than by post. This politically correct comment was enough to allow my student to classify his teacher ideologically and predict her opinions on most issues. My student reported to me that her bias was resented by many members her class. But my student saw this differently, as an opportunity. He cleverly exploited this knowledge for his internally assessed assignments and then he cleverly exploited the bias of the system with equal vigor during the externally assessed final exams. This brought him a well-deserved 86% for English. As he said, it was 'in the bag'.

There is something else that you need to consider when classifying the ideological biases of academics. At the tertiary level, the biases of lecturers or tutors are usually understood in terms of theoretical frameworks or scholarly traditions. Rather than define their approaches simply as Marxist or feminist, you would instead classify them as working within, for example, a Marxist or feminist theoretical framework or tradition. You should be aware that while some academics are theoretically pure or orthodox, most prefer to combine complementary traditions or frameworks in various combinations. You should also note that within broad traditions such as Marxism there is a myriad of minor schools of thought. In addition, since the dismantling of the Berlin wall and the collapse of communism in Eastern Europe, many Marxists no longer label themselves as such, disguising or refashioning their identities under designations such as 'structuralist' or 'post-structuralist', with many having leaped head first, along with many other leftist academics and a few others, into the theoretical labyrinth of postmodern social theory.

Despite this, there are a few simple methods you can use to classify them if your philosophical knowledge is not yet sophisticated enough to determine this from what they say in class. If they have not openly declared their preferred theoretical framework in a lecture or tutorial then you may be able to detect it by closely examining their prescribed course reading guide to identify a bias in the choices of reading materials. You can also find clues in the way the essay questions are framed, particularly if they require you to follow certain methodologies that pertain to particular theoretical frameworks. If you remain puzzled, you should look up the academic who is your examiner in the library and explore the articles or books they have published to determine the theoretical framework that they used. Then you can also use it and, by doing so, identify yourself to them as aspiring to be a member of their scholarly community, a move that will bring immediate benefits to your assessment. In fact you can go further than this.

Unlike teachers, most academics have published articles or books on relevant areas of study. Because of this, there is a powerful technique that tertiary students can use that is not available to secondary students. Whenever it is possible to do so, I recommend to my tertiary students that they read their examiner's publications on the topic then rely heavily on them to answer the essay question. While doing so, the student deliberately shows an appreciation for the academic's 'valuable' contribution to this field of inquiry. This technique combines the principle of deriving the content of your essay from your examiner's understanding of the topic, as recommended following the analogy of the 'black shoe', with the appreciation of the psychological effects that result from reflecting the ideological bias of your examiner. The result is the most awesomely powerful mix of persuasive techniques you could employ, the study skills equivalent of a cruise missile. Academics are sages who crave recognition and appreciation for the products of their mind. With this method it is possible to craft your essays to fill your examiner with such momentous uplifting intellectual validation that they will award you the highest grades with enthusiasm. Nevertheless, when you use this powerful technique there is a risk that you must avoid. You must interpret their work accurately. Mistakes will cost you because they will be perceived as an insult. If you have the opportunity to use this technique, seize it, because not only will you win, you will win handsomely.

Values

While it is possible to determine with reasonable accuracy the ideological bias of both your unseen and seen examiners, this is not the case in regards to their values. To do this effectively you need to either directly observe your examiners or gather information from someone who has. Although many sociologists and political scientists use the term values in a fashion that would encompass ideology, I am using it in a different manner, to cover important additional inclinations and preferences that do not fit into the category of ideology. This could include an appreciation of recreational cycling, gardening, attending the theatre, spectator sports, or the satisfactions that come from raising a family.

To appreciate the role that an understanding of your teacher's values can play in your success I have to explain to you the nature of rapport. Rapport refers to the feelings of like-mindedness, affinity, or mutual connectedness that form the basis of friendship. Rather than attributing rapport to 'chemistry' and thereby leaving it to chance, you should recognise that rapport can be engineered. People like like-minded people, those with whom they share things in common. If you demonstrate that you share significant likes and dislikes with your teacher (who is also your examiner) then you have increased the likelihood that they will care about or, better still, favour your success, simply because they like you. It will also help you to avoid the chance of an indifferent, uninterested or negligent treatment of your work that could be detrimental.

Furthermore, there are important additional uses for this information about their values. You can use it to carefully construct your essays to ensure that their topics and content are perfectly and precisely tailored to maximise their appeal to your examiner. To illustrate to my students the competitive advantage that they can enjoy if they tune into their examiner's values I ask them to think of their ten favourite films. I then say to them that I am sure that these films were superbly directed, performed, and had outstanding production values. Then I add, but so do hundreds of other films. These other excellent films are equally accomplished but they do not number in your top ten. Why? The reason is because in addition to their quality there was something in the subject matter of your top ten films that touched you personally. Other students may compete in class by trying to produce essays of greater quality than those of their rivals, but if you produce work that is both of high quality and in tune with your examiner's values your work will not simply be awarded high grades, it will be awarded the highest grades because it will be among the favourite essays that your examiner has ever corrected. Now that is an advantage!

This advantage has been appreciated by most of my students, including one of my year 12 English students who showed himself to be particularly skilled at the Method. I initially met this student at the close of his year 11. At our first meeting, while helping him to improve his analytical skills we, from time to time, paused and chatted about what interested my student and his ambitions. Although still a little shy, he modestly shared with me techniques that he had developed to improve his odds while betting at the racetrack. Wow, I thought to myself, this person has already demonstrated his ability to succeed. We just need to transfer it from the racetrack to the classroom. Later, his mother told me that she hoped that with my help her son would improve to receive a 'B' for English. I confidently told her that we would do much better than that.

My student took to my study method with enthusiasm and he conducted his espionage well. During one of our lessons my student reported to me that while he was consulting his teacher to receive his comments on a piece of work, he noticed on his teacher's desk an affectionate note the teacher had written to himself to remind him to do an errand for his son. My student immediately realised that the father and son relationship was extremely important to this man. Consequently, my student chose as the topic for the first essay in his creative writing portfolio to write a touchingly sentimental piece about a son who tenderly professes his love for his father while at his hospital bedside. In addition, my student had also noticed that his teacher used many sporting metaphors to illustrate his lessons. Aware that this indicated that his teacher had a love of sports, my student, for the remaining pieces of his writing portfolio, wrote essays that celebrated the joys of following spectator sports. My student received the highest marks for his writing portfolio. His teacher was so impressed that he praised my student for the extent to which his work had improved on previous years. At the end of the year, my student received 80%, his first 'A' for English. My student was delighted and his mother was very proud.

Ethics

In addition to noting the values of your examiners, you should also determine their ethics. The philosophical terms 'ethics' and 'morality' both refer to concepts about right or wrong. They are usually expressed as 'should' statements, such as people should do this or should not do that. When observing people's ethics, you will find that they are usually, but not always, closely related to their ideology and values. **In addition, you should be aware that many people can be quite passionate about matters that they perceive in ethical terms, becoming quite favourably disposed to those whom they perceive as sharing their**

ethics and negatively disposed or hostile towards those whom they perceive as contravening their ethics. Consequently, you should be careful to avoid appearing to go against your examiner's ethical principles. There are two possible consequences, and neither of them are particularly advantageous. If, for example, a teacher subscribes to a morality derived from Catholicism, then it is highly unlikely that their students will be awarded an 'A' for essays that advocated either contraception, abortion or artificial insemination, because to do so would simply go against the teacher's ethical conscience. For these teachers, to award an 'A' to such an essay would be virtually impossible because it would seem in their imaginations to be expressing approval for beliefs to which they may be uncompromisingly opposed. The worst consequence for students who contravene their teacher's ethics is the risk that the teacher will regard these students as morally bad people and consequently perceive their actions and submitted work from a perspective that predisposes them towards disapproval.

On the other hand, if you cleverly show yourself to share your examiner's ethical principles you can find yourself handsomely rewarded in grades. There are excellent opportunities to do this if your teacher asks you to write an essay that outlines your philosophy of life or describes your hero. Many students regard a request to write an essay about their philosophy of life to be an unfairly intrusive invasion of their privacy. Instead, you should see this as an excellent opportunity to establish rapport and show an ethical affinity with your examiner. From your notes on your teacher's psychological profile you should be well acquainted with their philosophy of life, so you simply present your teacher's philosophy of life pretending that it is your own. Similarly, if you have to write about your hero, you simply use your psychological profile of your examiner to create a fictional character, such as a favourite aunt, then you imbue that character with idealised descriptions of the qualities and beliefs of your teacher. Some of my cheekier students have even gone so far as to have given these fictional characters the physical characteristics of their teacher, as well as describing their hero as having, for example, a hatred of racism and a strong sense of charity. These students received 'As', after all, what other grade could they award to an essay about such a wonderful person?

Interests

In addition to ethics, there is the category of interests, which does not refer to the hobbies or pastimes that are dealt with under the category of values. This category refers to how people derive their incomes. The way that people derive their income often profoundly affects how they think about particular issues. **People, including your educators, can be very protective about the legitimacy of how they make their money, and this protectiveness can influence their treatment of others.** Teachers are salaried tertiary-educated professionals who are mostly employed in the public sector, with the exception of those who work in private schools. You may have noticed that those teachers who are employed by the government often support the principle that education is a right that should be provided free by the state, while those teachers who work in the private sector may have a different view. You should be aware that if you criticise or mock the teaching profession you are probably perceived as showing disrespect for the source of their income and undermining the legitimacy of their interests. Avoid the temptation to make those snide little jokes that many students make about teachers or school, either in conversations with teachers or in essays. You may see these remarks as 'innocent' and hope that the teacher will laugh with you. Unfortunately, while they may appear to laugh along with this humour made at their expense, they are probably concealing less appreciative sentiments that could compromise their feelings towards the source of this irreverence. Furthermore, if you were truly honest with yourself, you would admit that these jokes are usually manifestations of suppressed resentment, and it is in your best interest that this should be expressed in some more innocuous fashion.

A career in teaching or academia is for many a vocation with intrinsic rewards that have nothing to do with remuneration. Consequently, a number of teachers or lecturers can perform competently or excellently regardless of how much they are paid, simply because it is in their nature to do so. Unfortunately, others can become jaded and increasingly uninterested, especially some of the tenured lecturers, or those teachers who are protected by a powerful militant union, who realise that they are paid the same whether they do a good or a bad job. My recommendation to you that you take responsibility for your own education is partly based on a recognition of the implications of the reality regarding the interests of your educators. With some of your educators you may simply have to realistically lower your expectations.

You should also appreciate that most university tutors are paid at a sessional rate, which means that they are contracted casually and paid for their class contact time and not for the preparation of a lesson. Therefore there is no financial incentive for them to do much more than listen to the students' presentations of tutorial papers and then attempt to stimulate a discussion. In addition, they are not paid extra to provide students with advice or help, even though they are expected to do so. Moreover, most of them are postgraduate students who value every moment they can spend on their studies, so they often become concerned about the extent to which their tutoring cuts into their study time. Many tutors agree to this economic exploitation because they see it as an honour to have been appointed and as a necessary step towards an academic career. These financial disincentives help to explain why some tutors can seem to be less helpful than you expected them to be. Nevertheless, it is also the case that a number of your tutors will, despite their low pay, provide their students with well-prepared richly informative tutorials, as well as valuable advice and support simply because they are talented people who are naturally inclined to be helpful. I advise you to sign up for their tutorials rather than those of other tutors.

Another way that the interests of academics can influence your education and assessment is if student demand for a particular subject or course drops, thereby threatening the future of the subject or course and therefore the careers of the academics who are employed to teach it. Student demand can depend on the intrinsic interest or topicality of the course, or its value for students in improving their future employment prospects. It can also be influenced by the quality of the lecturer or even whether students perceive the lecturer as an easy or hard marker. Consequently, some lecturers, who are under pressure, may find themselves grading their students' essays and exams easier to avoid alienating the potential enrolments who are needed to keep themselves in employment. When this situation is evident, you may find it advantageous in your pursuit of high grades.

Preferred forms of language

In addition to becoming aware of your examiners' interests, it is important that you also determine their preferred forms of language, that is, those forms of expression that they prefer to reward and that you therefore need to use when dealing with them. You can determine your teacher's preferred forms of language by listening attentively in class to the kinds of expression that they use. Other clues will be evident if they provide the class with examples of writing that they admire, or in their critical responses to the expression you used in your initial items of submitted work.

Many teachers like big pretentious words, while some teachers prefer simple widely accessible words; some teachers like self-conscious flowery descriptive language, while others like precise language. You will need to become stylistically flexible and versatile. So, if your English teacher likes big pretentious words then those are what you will profitably use with this teacher, while if your History teacher prefers precise language then that is what you will profitably use with that teacher. Importantly, you should also listen for your teacher's pet words and phrases, such as 'bilateral relations' or 'juxtaposition', then use them in your essays as often as you can. This technique is powerfully effective at creating the positive feelings in your examiner that are conducive to the awarding of high grades.

This is because this linguistic mimicry is generally appreciated at a subconscious and emotional level rather than in an objective rational fashion. It represents a subtle form of psychological mirroring that can bypass the conscious mind and register in the unconscious by generating endearing heartwarming feelings of affinity. If you use their own forms of language it subtly suggests to them that you are tuned into their way of thinking. They will feel flattered, proud, satisfied and possibly secretly delighted that they have made a significant impact on a young mind. So do not be afraid to use their language because you fear that it may seem too obvious. With this technique, it is the case that he who dares wins. As many of my students have already discovered, you will probably find that the biggest ticks on your corrected assignments are found precisely where you mimicked your teacher's language.

You should also be aware that there are forms of language that you should avoid. Most teachers have hostile reactions to the use of simple words like 'got' or to the use of contractions like 'don't' in the place of the words 'do not'. So do not use these words in your submitted work. At best, you risk having your examiner wince with annoyance and possibly feel justified in subtracting marks for poor expression. At worst, your use of these words may trigger in your examiner a critical frame of mind that can prejudice their appreciation of your argument and analysis.

The form of language that is rewarded most at school and is a prerequisite for success at university is what is described as scholarly English. This is the learned prose that is found in academic books and journals. It is the style that is generally associated with the expression of intelligent ideas. Scholarly language is moderate, reasoned, precise, and it obeys the conventions of formal English. In addition, it generally avoids colloquial or emotive language and is comfortable with the appropriate technical terminology of the subject being discussed. Scholarly language is arguably the most appropriate form of expression for effectively communicating clever ideas and you should devote yourself to becoming competent in its use by imitating the better examples of it that you will encounter in your studies. Nevertheless, you should be aware that your teacher's preference for it may be, in part, irrational. In reality, clever ideas can be expressed in many forms of English, even broken English, and still be clever ideas. Some examiners' preferences for scholarly English can amount to a prejudice that is just as irrational as the assumption that financial advice is more reliable when delivered by someone wearing a business suit rather than jeans.

It is important for your academic success that you should become competent in using scholarly language but beware of the danger of succumbing to its dark side. Scholarly language should become another arrow in your quiver and not your sole form of expression. It is inappropriate for use in the school yard or for chatting in the kitchen with your grandmother, unless she is a professor, and then only for discussing certain subjects. In addition, you need to avoid slipping into the trap of producing scholarly language that is pretentious, jargon-laden, and difficult to decipher. Remember that your examiners are human beings who, like most people, appreciate text that is clear, legible, and enjoyable to read, as well as being scholarly.

Character

While taking notes on your educator's preferred forms of language, you were paying attention to how they communicated rather than what they said. Similarly, while taking notes on the character of your educator, it is more profitable for you to note what they do rather than what they say about themselves. **Your notes on the character of your educators help you to determine the kind of people with whom you are dealing, and therefore form appropriate strategies.** Interestingly, you are probably already taking mental notes along these lines to reach conclusions about whether your teachers are, for example, reasonable or unreasonable people. I am simply asking you to do this more systematically for constructive purposes.

Firstly, you need to determine whether or not your teachers are fair and broad-minded. To do this you observe how they respond to the contributions of students who offer answers that differ from the teacher's interpretation. If they are dismissive, then this is not the class where you will be rewarded for original ideas so you may have to adopt the strategy of reflecting the teacher's opinions in your assignments to receive your 'A'. You also need to determine whether or not they are a 'rule worshipper'. A rule worshipper is someone who believes that people serve rules rather than rules serve people. For example, if your English teacher is a rule worshipper then you must make sure that your assignments are always ready on time because this person is unlikely to grant you an extension. If you are pressed for time while doing several assignments, it would be best to ask for an extension from your History teacher who has a different attitude to rules; then you complete your English assignment before returning to your History homework. It also matters whether your teacher is an easy or hard marker. If you have a hard marker then you will have to ensure that your work measures up to their more exacting standards. You also need to take note of whether your teachers are willing to help students outside of class time. If they are, then avail yourself of this assistance if it is required. In addition, some teachers are egotistical and must always have the last word while others must always feel that they are right. If you have one of these, humour them. On the other hand, if you notice that your teacher has a sense of fun, then you know you can share a joke with them. You must also determine whether they treat people reasonably equally or blatantly play favourites. If they do play favourites then you need to determine the basis upon which these favourites are selected and then become one.

In addition to these points, there are many other potentially significant dimensions of the natures of your educators that could come under the category of character. It will be up to you to be observant so you can identify what is important enough to note and acknowledge. But before we move on to discuss the category 'persona', I would like to share with you some additional insights to help you understand how and why your examiners may respond differently to different forms of information or arguments that may be in your assignments.

The fact/value dichotomy

While observing human behaviour during political debates I have noticed that people seem to conceptualise 'the truth' in either of two ways, on the basis of consistency with empirically verifiable facts (objectively) or on the basis of consistency with the ideology, values and ethics that constitute the core of their world view (normatively).

All of us are both factual and normative to some degree when determining the truth. We all have ideologies, values and ethical beliefs that shape our perception of the world and the phenomena in it, and we can all appreciate objective facts. Despite this, you can also observe that some people seem to be more likely to use ideology, values and ethics to determine the truth and consequently be more likely to devalue or dismiss inconsistent facts. Meanwhile other people may be, by contrast, more inclined to put a premium on verifiable facts and consequently more inclined to devalue or dismiss ideologies, values, and ethical principles that are inconsistent with the relevant facts. I believe this dichotomy, or division, which I have called the fact/value dichotomy, broadly classifies two kinds of mindsets and therefore two kinds of people. Consequently, it helps us to understand and explain their divergent responses to various issues, debates, data and arguments. The fact/value dichotomy, which is similar to the historically well-known faith/reason dichotomy, can also be used to understand the thinking behind your examiners' positive or negative responses to arguments or facts that you included in an essay or exam. With the fact/value dichotomy at your disposal you may be able to avoid an examiner's negative responses and maximise their positive responses by taking care to formulate your argument in the fashion that they appreciate.

The fact/value dichotomy can be observed in many public debates. But to help you to understand it so you can use it to your advantage, I shall describe one of these debates where I believe it was illustrated with instructive clarity. In New York, a bronze statue was commissioned to commemorate the heroic patriotism of three firemen who defiantly raised the American flag in the aftermath of the devastating terrorist attack, on 11 September 2001, that demolished the Twin Towers and killed hundreds of civilians and many of the firemen who struggled valiantly to save them. The official statue reflected the ideology of political correctness (specifically anti-racism and multiculturalism) and depicted the three firemen as one white, one Hispanic, and one black. In reality, all three of the firemen involved in the actual historical incident were white, belonging to a fire department that was ethnically predominantly white.

Now the notion of the inter-ethnic brotherhood expressed by many New Yorkers in the face of this adversity is a historically defensible claim, and many examples of it could be found to support the kind of sentiment expressed in the statue; yet the decision to express this sentiment in a statue that distorted the factual reality of an actual event is what highlights the distinction between the two mindsets that are defined by the fact/value dichotomy. To those people who put a premium on facts, the statue's historical misrepresentation was an outrage. Interestingly, many others exhibited no concern about the empirical facts, believing that the statue reflected a (more abstract) thematic truth that contained a message that was more important than the mere facts about the real ethnicity of the firemen. To those who see virtue as, in part, involving a factual honesty, this statue could be regarded as lamentably unethical. Meanwhile, those who perceive virtue in terms of adherence to a particular ideology, values or ethical principles, the statue would be commendably ethical. Furthermore, they may possibly see the criticisms of the statue as disturbingly unethical, perhaps even as an attack on the ideology, values and ethical principles from which they derive their sense of truth and virtue.

The adherents of each of the mindsets that are distinguished by the fact/value dichotomy can have difficulty appreciating the opinions of those who have the other mindset to their own. Consequently, some students may have experienced an unexpected and startlingly hostile response from a politically correct teacher or lecturer to an essay that was simply concerned with exploring the facts. Interestingly, most people from each mindset tend to assume that everyone else forms their opinions on issues in the same manner as they do. As a result, those who put a premium on facts can see those who fall on the value side of the dichotomy as bizarre, even crazy, hence the use of derogatory terms like 'loony Left'. Meanwhile, those who see truth and virtue determined largely through allegiance to a particular ideology, values or ethical principles often assume that their opponents on a particular issue have not taken that position because the facts pointed in a particular direction. Instead, they believe that they must subscribe to a rival nefarious ideology, and the references to the facts are merely a rationalisation for dark sentiments reached by other means, hence the tendency to sweepingly accuse the critics of a multi-racial statue of 'redneck' racism.

You should also be aware that not all debates take place along the axis of the fact/value dichotomy. Instead, they can occur within either side. There are often debates between the advocates of different facts. Meanwhile, debates also occur between the advocates of rival ideologies, values and ethical systems, which interestingly can often quickly become passionate and ruthless, as is evident in the conflict between political correctness and traditional nationalism. Consequently, if a student, whose mindset falls on the value side of the dichotomy, promotes an ideology that is different to that of an examiner whose mindset also falls on this side, he may find himself arousing a disproportionately critical and unpleasant response to his assignments.

Interestingly, many of the people who would fall on the value side of the fact/value dichotomy would resent such a classification. In the academic world, many of these people proclaim themselves to be objective scholars. They could, if challenged, recall many occasions when they appreciated facts and this would be for them sufficient reason to stridently deny that they usually favour norms over facts. As I have said to you before, observe people's behaviour rather than what they say about themselves in order to determine their nature. You will find that in practice these people often treat facts as debating points rather than as steps to greater understanding. In addition, as each fact in their armory is disproved in the debate, they usually move on to use another fact and continue their assault rather than pause and reflect on the implications these disproved facts may have for their position.

The fact/value dichotomy can give you considerable insight into how your examiners tick, specifically how they may process certain data and arguments. You will find that if your examiners fall on the fact side of the dichotomy, they may be more appreciative of empirical arguments or new research discoveries. Those who fall on the value side of the dichotomy are more likely to appreciate theoretically based arguments that are consistent with their underlying fundamental principles or new theories that are even more in tune with these fundamental principles.

It is important to note that although I have used an example to explain the fact/value dichotomy that highlighted political correctness as falling on the value side, the adherents of most other ideologies could also be classified in the same fashion, whether they be economic rationalists, nationalists or the supporters of the Christian Right. I have singled out political correctness for special attention, here and elsewhere in the book, because it is the dominant ideology in the Australian education system and the one that you are most likely to encounter. Interestingly, the same could be said of the situation in many other education systems in the Western world. The fact/value dichotomy, and the other techniques in this book, are ideologically neutral. They can help you to deal with a system dominated by political correctness or any other ideology. They can help you to deal with examiners who may have a politically correct bias or any other form of bias.

Persona

In addition to taking notes on the character of your educators, it is necessary to determine their persona. The image, or persona, that people project to the world often affects how they see themselves in it. **People, including your educators, like to have their persona validated and reinforced by their environment, and they can be acutely sensitive to comments or actions that either support or undermine their public image.** For example, some teachers like to project an image that is young at heart. Meanwhile, some students may regard their teacher as not so young anymore and succumb to the temptation to make a sarcastic remark. Be warned. These comments are more emotionally hurtful to teachers than many students assume, even though teachers may give the impression that the remark was as inconsequential as water off a duck's back. Such comments may damage the rapport between the teacher and the student that is advantageous in terms of receiving high grades from this teacher. On the other hand, if students' comments and behaviour reinforce the teacher's persona, they tend to look favourably on these students.

Some educators are stylish while others simply dress rather than dress up. Some educators see themselves as intellectuals while others see themselves as athletically rugged. Some see themselves as respectable citizens while others are more casual or easy going. The persona of some educators may be fairly robust yet with some others it may be connected to a particularly fragile sense of self-esteem that could easily be inadvertently compromised by a student, as one of my year 12 English students discovered.

My student, who was a young woman with fashion model good looks, was determined to qualify to study Law, a course that required from students the highest university entrance scores, so there was no margin for error. Her father was a successful lawyer and her ambition was to honour him by following in his footsteps. My student began her campaign by compiling a psychological profile of her English teacher. Each piece of work that my student completed was carefully calculated to be in tune with the teacher's bias as well as her understanding of the subject matter, and as a result the 'As' rolled in as hoped. When my student had to produce a portfolio of creative writing she decided to include as her final piece a whimsically humorous essay about supermarkets, with one of the most entertaining paragraphs being about what the contents of peoples' shopping trolleys reveal about them, especially as to whether they are fit and lean or otherwise. I had observed that this essay was of a very high standard and likely to maintain the 'A' grade average that my student required, yet the reaction of her teacher surprised us both. She rejected the essay completely, refusing to grade it at all, ordering my student to produce another. My student, commendably, did not panic in the face of this apparent maltreatment. We turned to the psychological profile of her teacher for answers. The teacher was not much older than her students, this being her first year of teaching, and by contrast to my student she was overweight. What neither of us realised at the time was her acute sensitivity about this issue and that she had the potential to misinterpret some of the content of my student's essay as a personal attack on her appearance.

One of the strengths of the Method that my students use is its flexibility. If there is a miscalculation, they simply recalculate then renew their campaign. My student updated the psychological profile on the basis of her enriched understanding of her teacher's human frailty and the dynamics of the interpersonal situation between them. She then produced an essay that ridiculed the shallow character of an aspiring beauty queen called Cinderella. My student received her 'A', and later qualified to study Law. Just think, this student's ambitions could have been thwarted by the low self-esteem of one teacher. Luckily, this student's command of the Method had underscored her resilience and assisted her to achieve her final triumph. By the way, my student did pursue a modelling career, as well as studying Law. Although I am happy for her, I also think of the many other students who, unaware of the Method, were ill equipped to navigate the psychological minefield that can exist in their examiners and, sadly, they paid a price that could have been avoided.

As indicated in this and other examples, you should, after about a week of compiling notes on your educator (who is your examiner) under the categories of ideology, values, ethics, interests, preferred forms of language, character, and persona, construct a psychological profile of your examiner, which will be a list of points about a page in length. You can, of course, update this list throughout the year as required. Importantly, your command of this information is vital if you are to generate the feelings in your examiner associated with the awarding of 'As'. You will use this profile to calculate the choice of topics and content of your essays to maximise their likelihood of producing consistently high results. If you make a mistake, you simply modify the psychological profile as required then renew your efforts in accordance with these changes. As a result of using this method, your odds for achieving success should dramatically improve.

The Method in action

The following examples illustrate the effective use by students in concerted campaigns of many of the techniques that I have discussed. These students' experiences should help you to appreciate how you too can put these techniques to use to maximise your chances for success in the education system. The first of these students came to me early in his year 11. He was wanting to improve his grade average in English from 'Bs' to 'As'. I noticed from the examples of his work that he showed me that he was clever and had a flair for writing, which I would seek to develop. I also introduced him to the Method. His teacher had taken the class to see the film *Shakespeare in Love*, and his first assignment was to write a review. I taught my student how to write a film review, and he learnt quickly. I also warned him that the teacher would not seek and receive permission to take her class to see a film that she did not regard as particularly special. Even though my student was indifferent to the movie, he realised that he had to write a positive review. He did more than this, using his psychological profile of his examiner his review celebrated precisely the aspects of the film that would have appealed to his teacher, highlighting the film's earthy portrayal of Shakespeare as a cool, handsome, sexy young man, as well as its feminist treatment of gender issues. By being perfectly in tune with his examiner's bias, my student's essay induced in her the non-critical frame of mind that is conducive to examiners not even noticing a student's little mistakes. Despite this advantage, the review was so well written that there was little that his examiner could have criticised. My student's first essay achieved more than an 'A'. It put him at the top of the class and established a rapport with his teacher by suggesting that they were kindred spirits who liked the same film for the same reasons. It did more than this, it encouraged my student's teacher to pick him as one of those whom she regarded as a prime candidate for an 'A' at the end of the year, which she enthusiastically told my student's delighted parents at the parent-teacher interview that followed shortly afterwards.

Indeed, this student was ideally positioned for success. He had established the persona of the keen, diligent, capable student, this being the kind of persona that teachers like to reward. He was closely in tune with his teacher's bias, so much so that it had helped to generate rapport so the teacher cared about my student's success. Moreover, she had picked him as a winner, and since she graded all the students' work, she was the one with the power to bring about this prophecy. In addition, my student had also increased the quality of his work, so it exhibited the merit that deserved to be rewarded with high grades.

Interestingly, unknown to this student, another student from the same class contacted me requiring assistance because, unlike this first student, his year was off to a bad start. Like the first student, this second student was also very clever and capable. Even though this second student supported the Australian Labor Party, he was irked by his teacher's obsessive political correctness. He had even argued with her over the subject. 'Why can't I use the word boong', he goaded. 'Because it is insulting to black people', she uprightly replied. 'But I'm black and I'm not offended', my student cheekily retorted. He is a dark-skinned Indian. I winced sympathetically when my second student told me this story. It is often easy to score a verbal point off a teacher. Unfortunately, due to the power imbalance in the teacher-student relationship, the teacher can later seek her revenge through the way she assesses the student's work. Like my first student, this student had also been asked to write a review of *Shakespeare in Love*. He did not share his teacher's enthusiasm for the film and his opening lines revealed that this was a damning review where he argued that it would have been better had the film never been made. Ouch! With his teacher already prejudiced against him, my second student had worsened the situation by crossing her bias. Consequently, he induced in her what I term as the critical frame of mind, which meant that she scoured his work for every grammatical error for which she could deduct marks. His opening paragraph is covered with her corrections, some valid, others pedantic. But she did more than this. Right across the opening paragraph she brutally scrawled a line that viciously cut through his work. It seemed to have been made with such emotion that it appeared that his teacher had turned the pen around in her hand and angrily stabbed the page. Interestingly, she added only two minor corrections to the rest of the essay, indicating that she probably felt that she did not need to read much further than the opening to condemn this student. My second student had written an honest essay and received a low grade, much lower than he deserved, even though there were problems in the essay's structure and expression that required attention. It was the differing opinion of the student, and her already negative opinion of him, that had generated such a hostile response, not the quality of his work. Her behaviour also suggests that the merit exhibited in the essay of the first student was alone not enough to guarantee success. If he had not appreciated and exploited his teacher's bias his result may have been disappointingly different. These two students, who were both of approximately equal ability, provided an excellent scientific test to demonstrate the value of my method for succeeding in the education system. The test case, the first student, who had used the Method, was poised for success, while the control case, who was yet to learn and use the Method, was in a very difficult situation.

My first student only needed to continue doing what he was already doing to maintain his success, which he did. But with my second student, we needed to turn his situation around. My second student gathered information to compile a psychological profile of his examiner. He noted that in addition to being zealously politically correct, she was also an avid reader of popular psychology books about relationships and she liked to perform the role of den-mother to her class of teenage males by giving them advice on love and life. This provided us with a perfect opportunity. I advised my second student to write an essay that would tap into his teacher's nurturing sentiments so that he could become the focus of her sympathy. The class had been told to write a personal essay, which was supposed to be autobiographical. It was an assignment perfectly suited to our purposes. Aware of what was at stake, my student threw himself enthusiastically into the task. He took extra lessons with me so I could teach him some techniques on how to maximise the emotional impact of creative writing. He learnt quickly and fashioned an essay that was perfectly in tune with his teacher's values. It was a supposedly autobiographical story of a young man who had long desired a pretty girl whom he saw each day at the train station. When he eventually summoned the courage to say hello he received a humiliating knock-back that included a cruel insult about his looks. For this climactic final paragraph, my student seemed to have reached into his soul to find what was touchingly profound and moving language. I was very impressed. The essay had the desired effect on his teacher. Not only did she award an 'A', she was no longer hostile to him. This was encouraging but I felt that we needed to do more. My student came up with the idea for the next move in his campaign.

He was the head of a school club that consisted of students who were interested in politics who would sometimes organise speakers to visit the school. My student arranged for the East Timorese freedom campaigner, José Ramos-Horta, the Nobel Peace Prize winner, to speak at the school assembly. This man was one the heroes of my student's English teacher. After Ramos-Horta's visit, my student's teacher was joyously ecstatic. She was more than favourably disposed towards my student, she was trying to impress him. She now treated him as one of her most promising students. The unfortunate situation that had existed at the beginning of the year had been completely reversed and now my second student was poised for success along with my first student.

Coincidentally, later that year I was contacted by another student in that teacher's class. He too was unaware that I was tutoring his classmates. This student already exhibited the persona of the keen, diligent, capable student, so he required little advice in that regard. What he needed was to improve his essay writing skills, to learn how to capitalise on his teacher's bias, as well as to learn how to craft his work to match his teacher's understanding of the topic (following the lesson in the analogy of the 'black shoe'), which he did.

By the third term of the school year, I had three students in the same class, neither of whom knew that others were seeing the same private tutor. Interestingly, when they eventually realised what they shared in common, they formed a secret society, a secret society of the 'black shoe', where they would share information and tactics. They had terrific fun, and they each ended the year with 'As'. Interestingly, it was my second student, the one who began the year in such difficulty, who experienced the greatest end of year triumph of the three. His teacher was so impressed by his final exam that she presented it to the school Principal as an example of what she believed was exemplary work. This was quite a turnaround indeed.

Rather than being buffeted by fate, these students took responsibility for their education and succeeded. They used the advanced study strategies and tactics that I have explained to you, but they also used the fundamental study skills of effective research, essay writing and exam techniques that are required to lay the foundations for the successful use of these advanced skills. In a sense, it hardly matters whether or not students share the bias of their teacher if their work is around the 'D' or 'C' standards. At those levels, teachers are usually so preoccupied with the lack of fundamental skills of students that they care far less about their opinions. The situation changes once the competence of students reaches the 'B' or 'A' standards. At those levels their opinions are taken more seriously and additional factors come into the equation that mean that the improvements in knowledge and skills that facilitated the rise from 'C' to 'B' may not be sufficient on their own to reach and consistently maintain 'A' grades. Nevertheless, because competence in basic study skills is essential to lay the foundation for you to become successful, it is to learning them that we will now turn.

CHAPTER 3

SUCCESS THROUGH THE MASTERY OF BASIC, ADVANCED AND SUPER-ADVANCED STUDY SKILLS

Even though you have already been reading, note-taking and writing essays for many years, you will gain more from this chapter of the book if you approach it with an open mind, as if you are learning these skills for the first time. In this chapter, you will learn sound fundamental skills that can enable you to achieve the merit that will be a significant contributor to your success. In doing this, some of you may be building constructively on some of the skills that you have already learnt. Meanwhile, others among you may have to swiftly jettison many of the practices that you relied upon in the past. At this stage you are like a promising amateur athlete who has already enjoyed some success but has decided to go further to become a champion, a process of professionalisation that requires that you relearn most of your skills from scratch.

Rather than being an exact science, study is an art in which you will need to become proficiently skilled in all its dimensions. In this chapter of the book, you will be learning the art of planning and preparing your study campaign to position yourself for a successful year, as well as the art of effective reading and note-taking for a range of purposes. You will also learn the art of research and essay writing. In addition, this chapter will also cover public speaking, analysis and the other skills that you will need. As you learn, practise and eventually master these skills, your educational experiences will become more rewarding, both creatively and in terms of grades. In addition, many of these skills have wider applications than succeeding in the education system, helping you to benefit from and contribute to the world of knowledge as well as to express yourself effectively and profitably in many fields and endeavours.

Getting started: The art of planning, preparation and marshalling resources

A successful year of study requires careful planning and preparation to achieve your objectives, whether they be a high university entrance score, the high grades needed to transfer from the course you are currently doing to the one you really want to do, or to achieve the high grade average to qualify for postgraduate study, or simply to satisfy intellectual curiosity through enlightenment. Having determined your objectives, your campaign begins with an initial reconnaissance to find and obtain the information you need to position yourself to gain an overall strategic advantage. After you are advantageously positioned in the ideal course, subjects and classes, you then need to do further reconnaissance to develop more specifically focused strategic and tactical plans to succeed in your course and in each subject. Throughout this process of information gathering, planning and positioning, you should be marshalling the resources necessary to effectively execute your plans.

Course selection

Your initial reconnaissance sweep should start early, during the previous year or the summer holidays before the academic year commences. You may begin by consulting a career guidance officer or course adviser to help you access relevant information. From then, the process involves reading course and curriculum guide books, faculty handbooks, university guide books or school rule books. This usually makes for dry reading but you should persevere. What you are looking for are the crucial rules and regulations that will affect your progress: the key dates for enrolment, subject confirmation or discontinuation, the dates of examination and assessment, the criteria for special consideration, the requirements for promotion or graduation, etc. **This official course information gives you a sense of your options, and options mean choices, and choices contain the possibility of benefits because one choice may be more advantageous than another.** For example, you may learn that different year 12 subjects are weighted differently in how many points they can contribute to a university entrance score, with the more difficult traditional academic subjects, like Mathematics or History, being worth more than subjects like Environmental Science or Graphics. From this information, you can determine the subjects most likely to help you achieve your objective, thereby avoiding any unpleasant surprises when your grades are totalled at the end of the year. During this reconnaissance you may also discover opportunities to do subjects by correspondence that are not offered by your school, thereby widening your choices to include options that you otherwise believed were not available. Furthermore, by being aware of the dates when you can discontinue a subject, you know that if your progress is unsatisfactory you can drop it, thereby avoiding a blemish on your academic record, compensating later by picking up an extra unit next year.

Subject selection

Having clarified the scenario in which you will be operating, your next objective in your reconnaissance is to gather information about the nature of the subjects on offer and the educators who teach them as well as the expectations placed on the students who do these subjects. The official information found in curriculum and faculty guide books is useful but it should be complemented as much as possible with unofficial information about what these subjects and their educators are *really* like. Your best sources are other students who have completed those subjects and have first-hand knowledge. Former students usually enjoy giving prospective students the 'low down' on subjects and lecturers, so these conversations will often be spiced with colourful anecdotes or unambiguously clear advice such as: 'Avoid her classes at all cost' or 'That subject is fantastic'. Some of this opinion can be found in the counter-faculty handbooks produced by student unions, or on websites where students post their reviews. Of course, this information is subjective, so you need to be careful as to how you weigh this advice. Opinions may differ widely among former students, and some ratings may simply be positive or negative depending on how that particular student fared rather than representing an objective summation of the quality of the subject. Be discerning. Remember, you own your decision and you will carry the consequences of taking it, not the people who advised you.

Your selection of subjects should be to make your strategic situation as advantageous as possible in pursuit of your objectives.

If your aim is to complete units that cover areas that encompass key intellectual or professional interests, then your selection may differ than if you are solely focused on maximising your grades. If you want to cover various interests, then carefully choose a range of subjects that touch upon as many of these as possible, so that the end result is a course that has the breadth that you require. Alternatively, you may choose subjects that overlap and complement each other, such as high school Politics and Legal Studies subjects that both cover democratic parliamentary procedure, or you may choose a university politics unit dealing with European fascism as well as a history unit on the Second World War that will both cover the study of the foreign policy of Nazi Germany. These choices will give your studies greater depth, since the reading for one subject can be used to enhance your performance in another.

Your selections of subjects to give your studies breadth or depth are rational choices. But when you are choosing subjects that will be central to your studies, some more instinctive decision-making processes may be necessary. When you are choosing the subjects in which you want to major, thereby taking them to the end of your undergraduate degree and possibly further, it can often help if you trust your gut feeling. It may make sense, for example, to study mathematics at a high level because it can increase your study or career options, but not if you do not have an aptitude for it and you have to struggle. Remember, subjects become more difficult each year. As you progress, you will eventually reach your limitations. If you spend too much time doing this subject then it may be a sign that your natural aptitude is elsewhere. Pick subjects that capitalise on your talents, with which you feel comfortable in your gut. If you can comfortably imagine yourself studying or practising this material for life, then you have made the right choice. If this thought makes you feel decidedly uncomfortable, then you may have to reassess your selection. In addition, the subjects that you are often best at and have the best chances of pursuing the farthest are usually ones that correspond with already apparent interests or hobbies. Alternatively, these subjects may correspond with potential interests that you are yet to develop, but may do so once you are formally studying in this area. These interests and potential interests can also provide you with clues as to where your most successful study directions may lie.

Selecting your educators

Once you have chosen your subjects, it makes sense to select your educators (if there are options available) because your choice of an educator is effectively a choice as to who will examine you for part or all of your assessment in a particular subject. As you are already aware, different examiners can vary dramatically as to their ability and attitudes, so you must plan and manoeuvre to maximise your prospects wherever possible. Unfortunately, at school there are very few chances to select your teachers. Yet, there may be opportunities in subjects with large enrolments where a range of classes (taught by a range of teachers) are staggered throughout the weekly timetable to compensate for potential timetable clashes, so virtually everyone interested in the subject can join a class. Similarly, there may be elective units within subjects that, again, involve different time table options for the same reason. While the school's main purpose for providing these options is to maximise subject choice, you can exploit this as an opportunity to select the better teacher among those on offer. You may opt for the easier marker, or the most dedicated and able, or the most open-minded and less biased of the alternatives.

At university there are greater opportunities to select your educators. When you commence a subject you are expected to promptly sign up for a tutorial. There will be a range of times from which students may select. Yet because different tutors will often be assigned to different tutorials, your selection of your tutorial is effectively also a selection of who will probably be your principal examiner. You should choose carefully to put yourself in the most strategically advantageous position. If you are unfamiliar with the options, ask other students for information about the tutors or, better still, shop around. Attend a couple of tutorials in the first week and test a range of tutors, then sign up with the one whom you prefer. If you become disappointed, then change tutorials. But be careful. Generally, lecturers and tutors do not like students to change tutorials, so you will need a good excuse because the truth will not suffice. Tell them that you had to change due to reasons of employment because a reallocation of work shifts has made your previous tutorial impossible to attend. Tutors and lecturers are themselves employees who work shifts, so they will be primed to identify with this predicament and appreciate this excuse.

Planning your approach

Once you have selected your subjects and educators, it is time to do your third round of reconnaissance. This time it is to devise the strategy with which you will approach completing this year's subjects. **You have to acquire a precise sense of what you need to do and when you need to do it.** By scrutinising your subject outlines and reading guides you may determine that, for example, for your four subjects you have to complete four major and eight minor essays, which is a total of twelve essays. You also have to prepare for four exams, each of which will involve another three essays. Because you discover that you can repeat in your exams the topics covered in your minor essays, this means that you only have to prepare another four different topics for examination. Altogether, you have to prepare and write on sixteen different topics.

You will soon realise, if you have not done so already, that time is one of your most valuable resources, so allocate it wisely. At university, you have about nine months from March to November to complete a specific number of tasks (while at school it is about ten months, from February to November). Within these parameters, you need to determine the due dates for the essays and the commencement dates for the exams. You also need to estimate the time it takes for you to complete a task, for example, two or three weeks to do an essay from start to finish. If, for example, you realise that three of the major essays are due at about the same time in the middle of the year, then you will have to stagger your commencement and completion of them so that they are all ready to be submitted by the due date; so you complete one well in advance, the second moderately in advance and the third just before the due date. If you notice that the submission dates for your final essays leaves only two weeks of clear time before the exams commence, which is not sufficient to prepare and study this volume of material, you will need to begin your preparations in advance, so that the two weeks available at the end of the academic year is all that you need to complete the process.

By devising a plan of action according to the number of tasks and the time that is available, you can schedule your studies to ensure that you are ready by the due dates for essay submission or examination. It can help if you note in your diary or calendar the dates of your own schedule along with the official due dates. Try to keep to your schedule, yet at the same time keep your plan sufficiently flexible, because some tasks may take longer and others less time than originally expected. In practice I have found that you may need to adjust your plan several times to accommodate unforeseen contingencies, and these contingencies usually put you a little behind schedule rather than ahead. So make allowances for this possibility by providing yourself with a few weeks of leeway near the end of the academic year that can be absorbed if required.

Organising your resources

While you are planning your study strategies you also need to be organising the resources necessary to achieve your objectives. One of the most important is a comfortable quiet work station. This can constitute a major financial investment, but it is well worth it. Firstly, you will need to find a quiet place in your home where you can work for long periods relatively undisturbed. Ideally, this place should be temperate (warm in winter and cool in summer), with a window that does not face the harsh morning or afternoon sun, which can be quite disconcerting, especially in summer. Secondly, you will need a desk with an adequate amount of surface space on which to lay the papers and books you may be using at any one time. Most importantly, this desk should be accompanied by a comfortable ergonomic executive chair, which needs to be adjustable, reclinable and fully supportive so you can completely relax without having to tense any muscles while you are seated. This degree of comfort is not a luxury but a necessity. It is necessary for good health, by protecting your back from the strain from working long periods in the same position. In addition, it will help you to avoid procrastination. If your chair is uncomfortable when used for long periods, this may not register clearly on your conscious mind as much as it does on your unconscious. The result will be that you will find yourself, despite your best intentions, making excuses to avoid commencing your studies: 'I'll start after this snack' or 'after this television program finishes' or 'after I have rested a little longer after such a gruelling day at school'. What is happening is that your body is looking for any excuse to avoid the pain that comes from sitting in an uncomfortable chair. The result is that valuable study time is lost. You should have a chair that is so comfortable that you look forward to relaxing in it as soon as you arrive home, thereby beginning your study almost immediately.

You will also need a computer with a printer and access to the internet. Most high schools and universities expect typed rather than handwritten essays, so the abilities to use word processing software and to type are essential. If you need to improve or acquire typing skills then you should do an adult education short course or purchase a software program that allows you to teach yourself. In addition, there are many computer manuals available that are written in clear, simple comprehensible English that will explain most software. If you familiarise yourself with some of these manuals you can find out more about the useful features that are available in your software, a number of which you may not have been aware. For example, most students profit from the spell-check function in the Microsoft Word tools menu but often do not fully capitalise on the grammar-check function that is also available. These features have major educational value because you can learn the grammatical rules as you correct your mistakes. By regularly using these marvellous features, over time, you will find yourself making fewer and fewer errors.

Internet access has also become vital for successful study by making a wealth of information available to you at your home. You will need to become familiar with key search engines, like Yahoo or Google, if you are not already, so you can access many informative web sites and pages, possibly bookmarking the most useful of them for easy future reference. You can also use the internet to check the availability of books and articles at your university library without leaving your home, or conveniently correspond with teachers or academics via email. In addition, the internet can often come to your rescue if you are in difficulty with a particularly challenging assignment, like poetry analysis. By looking up the poet and learning about his background and principal concerns, the poem in question may become more intelligible. You may even access reviews or analyses of the poem that orient you towards making sense of it. Thanks to the internet, this can all be achieved from the comfort of your work station.

Despite the value of these electronic information tools, reference books remain invaluable resources, and there are several acquisitions that are essential for your work station. The first is a quality English dictionary, which should be accessibly by your side at all times while you are working. Do not hesitate to look up the meanings of words that you do not understand or to clarify the meanings of words that you imperfectly understand. Most people do the former but not the latter, yet the latter will inform you of the various nuances of meaning that will make you more literate. An extensive vocabulary is a valuable resource and building this requires effort over time.

One way to improve your vocabulary more rapidly is to establish your own customised dictionary of words that you did not previously know. Allocate a folder for the task with pages designated from A to Z. When you look up a word that you do not understand, write all of its meanings and its pronunciation into your dictionary on the page headed by the first letter of the word. The effort that you take to write the word into your customised dictionary will help you to learn it. It should become part of your vocabulary as a consequence. If you continue reading and come across that word again, but its meaning unfortunately slipped from your memory, then quickly check it again in your customised dictionary. Initially, you may find yourself frequently looking up words and recording their meanings, but as your vocabulary improves you will need to look up words less often. After several years, when your vocabulary has dramatically improved, you may dispense with keeping your customised dictionary. But remember, the development of your vocabulary is a lifelong project. Continue to look up words, or ask people to define those terms that you need clarified.

While the English dictionary and the spell-check function on your computer will help you to correctly spell most words, they will usually not cover the names of people and places (including foreign names) that are specific to your subject. Luckily, if you have doubts about how to spell a particular name, there are resources at hand that are just as helpful as a dictionary. To find out how to spell the names of people and places, simply look them up in the index of a reputable book on the subject. Publishers usually take great care to ensure that names are spelt correctly, so you can capitalise on their endeavour to help you in your endeavour, by using the index of a book as a spelling dictionary.

Apart from an English dictionary, another reference that should be accessibly by your side is a style manual that clearly articulates the rules of grammar. The grammar-check feature in your computer's word processing software will help you learn from your mistakes, but the style manual will teach you the appropriate way to express yourself in the first place. You may use it to determine the formalities for making footnotes or endnotes, or to find out when to use single or double quotation marks, discovering that you use single quotation marks at almost all times and doubles when signifying a quotation within a quotation. Furthermore, it will inform that you do not use any quotation marks when a quotation is indented. You can use the style manual to look up specific rules as you need to know them. In addition to this, I recommend that you also find some time to read it thoroughly so you become more conversant with its contents. This will help you to develop a natural sense of what is grammatically correct that will, in turn, help to take the worry out of writing for those of you who are especially concerned about their expression.

Good spelling and grammar are important because they help you to communicate effectively, but do not let these concerns distract you from the flow of your ideas, which are of paramount importance to the quality of your writing. Well spelt, grammatically correct work is not necessarily good writing, merely well spelt, grammatically correct work. Good writing comes from the imagination and it is due primarily to the quality of your ideas. These ideas should be your principal concern while you are writing. You can sort out the spelling and grammar problems later. Unfortunately, you can only improve spelling and grammar gradually. In the meantime, you will still have to produce work. Reassure yourself that although English is a richly expressive and rewarding language to use, it is also very difficult due to its many irregular conjugations and words that are not phonetically spelt. In the context of this complexity, there is no shame in making a mistake or two, so do not let these slips compromise your morale. Nevertheless, you should not neglect this dimension of writing and let it languish because poor spelling and grammar can distract examiners from the appreciation of your ideas. Keep using your dictionary, style manual, and computer spell-check and grammar-check functions to become far more articulate and grammatically competent, so much so that you will eventually no longer regard yourself as someone with a problem in this area.

Meanwhile, another factor that can distract examiners from appreciating the quality of your ideas is the quality of your handwriting. While most submitted essays will be typed, the material produced in class, as well as during exams, will be handwritten. It is easy for a student's handwriting to become increasingly messy over time, especially due to the pressure to write quickly while taking notes in class. Sometimes this can reach a stage when the student's writing becomes quite difficult to read. When students submit messy handwritten pieces of work that are challenging to decipher, they usually hope that their teacher will persevere to find the gems of wisdom that lie buried in the messy script. This can happen, but so can the following. The messy handwriting puts the teacher into a critical frame of mind as they begin reading the student's work, so they assess it with an attitude that is already unfavourable. The teacher may begin by trying to scrutinise the writing, but become frustrated after encountering further difficulty, eventually resorting to skimming through the rest of the paper, neglecting to concentrate on it, thereby overlooking much of the content that the student hoped would bring reward. This student's grade will be an estimation rather than a calculation of its worth, and made in a state of antagonism at that. While your ability to write quickly is valuable for note-taking in class, it is also in your interests to have the ability to write clearly and legibly. This requires concentration, making sure that you form the letters correctly as you write them. If you have a problem with the quality of your handwriting, you should use some class work or assignments as opportunities to develop its clarity. Its legibility should improve immediately, and with practice the speed in which you can clearly form the letters should also improve.

Returning to the discussion of the reference books that you need to have on or near your desk, many students believe that a thesaurus should be one of them. A thesaurus is particularly useful for younger students who seek to broaden their vocabulary by being introduced to categories of words with similar meanings. Beware, these are usually words with *similar* meanings rather than the *same* meaning, contrary to what many students assume. Consequently, this reference should always be used in conjunction with a dictionary and never as an alternative to one. Using a thesaurus contains several dangers, and the mislearning of the meanings of words is one of them. There are others. Many students like the thesaurus because they can look up alternative word choices to avoid repeating a word in a sentence or paragraph, or they can find what seem to be impressively big or obscure words that they believe will convey the impression of stylish writing and high intellect. Unfortunately, what often results is an essay that is compromised by pretentiously obscure and inaccurate vocabulary. To avoid the dangers of 'thesaurus writing', students should use this reference sparingly and always in conjunction with a dictionary. While doing this, you will soon discover that it is usually more profitable to look up words in the dictionary first, where you will find that the dictionary definition can often provide you with an accurate alternative way of stating the same thing in different words, if that is the assistance that you require. Because of the dangers of thesaurus writing, the thesaurus should be seen more as an occasional rather than regular source of support in your expression, its educational value being, to some degree, transitional.

Having praised the English dictionary as a valuable reference one should also note its limitations. It does not provide the more detailed and elaborate explanations of the technical terms that pertain to particular subjects, like sociology, psychology, economics, etc., that lead to a more profound understanding of them. An English dictionary definition of a term from political philosophy, like 'liberalism', will describe what the word means but not reveal much about the concepts it represents. One way to learn more is to turn to specialised subject dictionaries. There are many to choose from, such as dictionaries of sociology, psychology, biology, philosophy, critical theory, Marxist thought, politics, modern history, historical terms, legal terms, religion, and many more. Of similar value are dictionaries of biography that allow you to look up notable writers, artists, scientists, statesmen, generals, etc. Other useful references include world guides that provide vital statistics and data on every country. Also of value are atlases, including historical atlases that reveal the different political geography during different periods, such as at the time of classical Athens or during the French Revolution, as well as almanacs or chronologies that cover particular eras or events, such as the twentieth century or the Vietnam War. The more of these types of books that you purchase, the more effective your reference resources will be. Because individual texts may vary in their comprehensiveness or in the detail provided in each entry, you may decide to purchase several on the same subject, so if one reference book does not resolve your particular inquiry, another may do so, or you may use several in combination.

General knowledge

You may turn to these specialised references when you require them to directly answer specific questions or, on other occasions, when you are under less pressure from impending assignments, you may choose to leaf through them at a more leisurely pace, pausing every so often to read various entries to satisfy your curiosity. If you do the latter, you may be adding to one of your most valuable resources – your general knowledge. General knowledge is miscellaneous information about a wide range of topics related to humanity and the natural world. It comes in several forms. It can consist of facts, such as that the dismantling of the Berlin Wall was in 1989. It can consist of explanations, such as how rival interlocking alliances contributed to the origins of the First World War. It can also be found in theoretical knowledge that can offer insights into a range of topics, such as psychological theories that help to explain certain forms of human behaviour. A broad general knowledge is a valuable asset for school or university study because it means that you know a little about a wide range of topics to enable you to talk intelligently about them or provide you with the initial grains of knowledge that you can develop into a more substantial body of knowledge. General knowledge is essential for answering essay questions in English, such as argumentative pieces about current events or creative writing about human nature. It can also help to orientate you towards more considered answers in a range of subjects, like politics, sociology, genetics or astronomy.

The acquisition of general knowledge does not happen overnight. It is a lifelong project that begins with an attitude. You need to be interested in, curious about and reflective upon the world around you, as well as willing to read, watch, and listen to informative media, literature and people to satisfy this interest and curiosity. General knowledge is acquired through appropriate habits rather than through intensive study, although study does add to the sum of ones general knowledge. **To acquire general knowledge you need to broaden your learning horizons beyond formal study. Make the world your university.** This involves keeping up with current events through quality news programs and journals. It also involves seeking out artistically distinguished or culturally significant films, music, art or literature as part of your leisure. It involves watching documentaries, reading books or talking to intelligent people who can provide knowledge or insight. This material can in turn enhance your appreciation of information derived from the news media by making it more intelligible and meaningful. Experience is another source of general knowledge, especially experience that has been reflected upon as to its significance and meaning. This can involve the experiences from family life, or relationships or employment or travel that provide anecdotes and lessons that can be used to make abstract theoretical material more comprehensible or to assess the credibility of evidence. Your studies will benefit because what you learn informally often rebounds positively on what you learn formally at school or university. The more that you know, the more comfortable that you become with learning new information.

The habits for continually acquiring general knowledge should become so ingrained that those who have them are barely conscious that they do. They are simply part of existence. Despite this, it should be acknowledged that the building of general knowledge should receive considerably less attention during the gateway years of study, when focus is required to obtain the grades to qualify to progress from high school to university or from undergraduate to postgraduate study.

Stationery supplies

Some aspects of your studies can become quite consuming and challenging, so intrusively so that while you are working on one project you find that your mind repeatedly switches to considering another more difficult one or that when you stop work at the end of the day you may find yourself still pondering unresolved problems. When this is the case, you need to be prepared for the possibility that the valuable ideas that can help to resolve these problems may come to you at any moment. Keep note pads at your desk, beside your bed, in the glove box of your car (if you have one), or in your pocket while you are shopping or walking the dog, in fact anywhere where you may need to quickly record an idea. This is because sometimes your best ideas occur when you are not directly engaged in study but doing something else. Similarly, a breakthrough idea for one project can sometimes come while you are working on another. If this happens, temporarily stop what you are doing and record these ideas on your handy note pad. Then label and store these ideas in a relevant place, such as by paper-clipping them to your notes for the other project, then you can resume the work that you interrupted. If a project is particularly inspiring, such as writing a major essay or thesis, you may find yourself thinking about it in your sleep. If this happens, sit up, grab the note pad and pen kept beside the bed for this purpose, record these ideas, then return to sleep, relaxed, knowing that these important ideas can profitably be incorporated into your draft the first thing the next morning. These ideas often constitute the solution to the problem that distracted your sleep in the first place. If you had not recorded these ideas on your handy note pad, you may have lost them.

As well as having a strategically placed note pad, your work station should also be sufficiently stocked with supplies of the stationery that you need, so if you run out of, for example, paper for you printer, you can conveniently draw from your stocks, thereby avoiding any interruption to your work. It is more efficient to periodically buy stationery to replenish your stocks rather than when your supplies are exhausted, an occurrence that can often happen at the least desirable moment, such as when a project is due and you are pressed for time. As well as being well supplied, your work station should also be reasonably tidy. A tidy desk reflects a tidy well-organised mind. Adhering to this principle involves keeping the materials and notes for your projects labelled and filed or piled neatly and separately, with library books stored in a different place to your own books, with their due dates recorded in your diary for prompt return or renewal.

Helpful allies

In addition to stationery and other equipment, a number of the resources that you will need to marshal for your success will be human, such as potentially helpful friends and associates at school or university, family members such as your parents, teachers or academics who perhaps taught you in previous years, expert librarians, or even private tutors. The more clever, capable, friendly and helpful people that you gather around you, the better off you will be. When you begin the academic year, you should have made an assessment of your strengths and weaknesses. You may seek to either compensate for or eradicate any limitations by drawing on the skills of others. This is one way you can follow the principle of making your weaknesses your strengths. Before I discuss this form of assistance further, I offer a word of warning. You will need to keep this assistance in proportion. In the long run, you will be better off if the balance between cooperative effort and self-reliance has the scales tipped much more towards self-reliance. Do not allow yourself to become dependent on the help of others. Generally, see this help as transitional or short-term or as a means to gain the knowledge and skills that will enable you to perform independently. If students become too needy and reliant on others it creates an internal dialogue of fear that is not conducive to success, so when these vulnerable students receive an assignment their first panicky question to themselves is who can I ask to help me do this? Your aim is to become a formidable student who can do a great deal for yourself but who may, when required, supplement or boost your strengths by drawing on the strengths of others. Curiously, you will notice that the more independently capable you are, the more willing others will be to help you, particularly experts. In addition, the more capable you are in your own right, the more capable you will be to help others and, due to the psychological law of reciprocity, the more willing others will be to help you, by returning the favour.

We have already learnt how other students can provide you with valuable information about the nature of courses, subjects and educators. They can do more. Classmates can lend you notes taken from classes that you may have missed when you were away sick, or they can quickly advise you about a helpful reference or point you towards the solution to a mathematical problem that has you temporarily baffled. School or university friends are in the same boat as you. They can therefore identify with your problems more readily and serve as a good sounding board to help you to let off steam if you are under pressure or feeling resentful after having been treated unfairly by a teacher. If you are establishing a support network of friends and associates, you should bear in mind the following principles. If you are supportive, friendly and helpful to others, generally they will be the same towards you. Secondly, if you want to be successful it helps if you associate principally with ambitious or successful people. If you seek out the company of the brightest and most dedicated students, their positive industrious attitudes can help to reinforce your own or inspire you to strive harder. In addition, clever friends can sometimes provide crucial assistance, such as if one of them takes the time to carefully explain to you an aspect of the subject that you did not understand. Clever friends can also be invaluable in emergency situations when, for example, an educator has mismanaged the teaching of a course leaving it improperly explained or incomplete in vital areas. In this situation, friends may be able to fill in the gaps by sharing their research notes that compensate for the mishandled or neglected topics. Similarly, if you fall perilously behind for whatever reason and the exams are looming, you may organise with friends to trade copies of notes or (assessed and returned) essays that are relevant to exam topics. This will help you to prepare when there was insufficient time for you to effectively do so on your own.

Having organised a number of supportive friends, it is generally best for study purposes that you meet with them individually, when necessary, rather than collectively as a study group. When working with one other classmate on clarifying a difficult dimension of a topic, it is easier to maintain your focus on the task at hand compared to if you were involved with a larger group. If you do form a study group, be wary. In many cases, they can be difficult to keep focused and disciplined. Although helpful at times, they are often prone to become sidelined by gossipy conversation that may be highly entertaining but of little academic benefit.

Other students are not the only people who can be profitably included in your support network. If you have established an appropriate persona, such as that of the keen, diligent, capable student or of the 'chip off the old block', this will be conducive to your ability to effectively consult some of your former teachers or academics for advice, for example, about additional references for a major essay. In this context, the assistance of an expert librarian may also prove to be invaluable in guiding you towards relevant sources for your research. While it is rare and rarely necessary for undergraduates to do so, postgraduate students may seek to network with relevant academics at other universities. Indeed, many academics expect and welcome such inquiries as part of the process whereby apprentice scholars (which is what postgraduate students are) become incorporated into the academic community. Nevertheless, you should bear in mind that academics are usually busy, so be tactful about how much you ask of them. If you require detailed expert assistance over time to compensate for the limitations of a particular educator or to provide supportive mentoring, then you may consider contracting a private tutor. When choosing, you should take into account that the most effective private tutors will combine formidable knowledge and intellectual ability with a caring helpful attitude. By contracting a private tutor, you can evade the educational costs of being allocated a 'dud' teacher that year or use the opportunity to dramatically improve your knowledge and study skills to obtain a competitive advantage in your pursuit of high grades.

The option of private tutors, along with the necessities of computers, reference books, etc., all cost money at a time when a student's study commitments put them in what is for most people their least financially viable phase of their life. If you are fortunate to have a supportive family and relatively stable home life, this can become one of the most valuable elements of your support network. Of particular value can be a student's parents or others who perform that role. Luckily for most students, most parents are more than happy to help their children succeed educationally. Sometimes they can become too involved, crossing boundaries into their children's privacy, but if they can see that their son or daughter is a diligent student it is easier to convince them to retreat because you have matters under control. Supportive parents can usually provide a comfortable and quiet study environment as well as moral support and encouragement. Parents or brothers or sisters may also check your drafts for clear expression or serve as an audience while you practise your oral presentation. If parents or other family members have the expertise, they may even help with more specialised dimensions of your study.

If your home life is less than ideal, the challenges that you face are more difficult but still achievable. There may be various sources of compensation that you could explore, such as potentially helpful grandparents or uncles or aunts or perhaps other caring people who may perform elements of the supportive role usually provided by parents. Remember, the more keen, diligent and capable that you seem to be, the more willing others will be to help you because they can see that their assistance will be put to good use.

Budgeting

Furthermore, many students move out of home while attending university, consequently parental financial support recedes to be replaced by increasing degrees of financial self-reliance. If this is the situation, you will need to pay attention to becoming adept at balancing work and study commitments, allocating limited resources, prioritising, and keeping to a budget, none of which are simple feats. Successful people are often identified by how productively they use their spare cash and their spare time, and this is as true of students as anyone else. In this sense, your capacity for focusing on your objective, delaying gratification and exercising self-discipline will be of paramount importance to avoid the financial pitfalls that can pressure students to abandon their course. It is important to find part-time or casual employment that can allow you to maximise the time that you can allocate for your studies, especially time when your mind is fresh and alert. Next, you may find it helpful to allocate your expenditure according to the following priorities. Firstly, cover your recurring survival costs such as rent, utilities, food, groceries and transport. Then allocate additional financial resources to cover less frequently occurring costs such as essential clothing. Similarly, your study expenditures should firstly cover your recurring costs such as stationery and photocopying expenses, before allocating resources to cover the less frequent expenditures on fees, textbooks or computer equipment. Extras, such as entertainment expenses, can be treated as rewards for following the priorities set out above. If it is possible to be thrifty to reduce costs or to save a little spare money to deal with unexpected expenses, try to do so, no matter how little these weekly savings may be. You could also establish sources from which you can borrow funds to deal with emergencies, such as family or friends or find out if your university offers low-interest or interest-free short-term student loans. More mature students, who have established businesses, trades or careers, may choose to prepare in advance for their course by saving a reserve of funds to cover them during leaner years of study when they will have less time to earn money. Similarly, other students with part-time or casual employment can do additional work during the summer holidays to accumulate a surplus that can be rationed throughout the economically leaner months. Living within limited means is difficult but possible. Some students may not consider this financial advice to be a study skill. Yet in the context of the considerable number of students who discontinue their courses due to financial difficulties, this is some of the most relevant advice of all.

Effective excuse letters

Before we move on to discuss other dimensions of the planning and preparation phase of your studies, we need to cover one more potentially beneficial element of having a family support network. You should be aware that while you are at school and living at home, parents can provide you with some of the most powerfully persuasive devices that you can have at your disposal – parental excuse notes, which are in effect a license to bend difficult situations to your favour when otherwise you would not have the opportunity to do so. The need for notes from your parents stems primarily from the school's supervisory responsibilities, with these notes being legal documents that are supposed to account for your whereabouts. Putting these legal dimensions aside, if your parents are supportive, parental notes can become almost magical enabling devices to provide you with extra study time at home to help you to meet assignment submission dates or better prepare for exams, with this extra time sometimes being decisive if you have fallen behind. This situation changes when you begin university. You will soon notice that university authorities will treat you as an independent individual and you can come and go as you please. Even though it is important to attend as many lectures and tutorials as possible, if you find that you cannot attend, for whatever reason, then you do not have to justify or explain your decision, except as a gesture of courtesy, which is your option to offer.

The main reason why excuses are required at university is for extensions to submit an assignment after the due date. Many academics are quite happy to give modest extensions, so requesting one will in many cases not be a formidable task. But be aware that it is possible that at some stage during your course, your future may hang in the balance depending on the effectiveness of an excuse letter as readily as it would with the passing of an exam. Consequently, to overcome these more significant obstacles you will need to become skilled at the art of persuasively expressing yourself both verbally and in formal letters. You will need to work on your case until you feel it is framed in such a way that it can achieve the task for which it is intended. To make it persuasive, you will need to think carefully about what the person in authority over you would like to hear or what they would say if they were in your situation, which at some stage in their past they have been, or at least something similar. You may consult other academics whom you know for helpful 'insider' advice in this regard. Make an appointment to meet with one of them, then ask something like the following: 'I have fallen behind doing my major essay in International Relations, and my degree may be hanging in the balance. I have to ask the Professor for an extension and I'm a little concerned about it. What do you think I should say to him that would be effective?' Then sit back and wait for him to tell you. Not only may you receive some valuable advice, but in the process of asking you may have recruited an advocate on the inside who may vouch for you to his colleague if your request runs into difficulty.

Your case for an extension will have a better chance of being persuasive if it does one or more of the following. It should be crafted to encourage your educator to identify with you or your predicament so they feel at some level that they are helping someone like themselves and will therefore feel good about themselves for having done so. You can also attempt to make your request seem so utterly reasonable that it is virtually impossible to find justifiable reasons with which to disagree. You may also frame your argument to seem as if it is in their interests as well as yours to agree to your request. In other words, you must include material that makes it easy for them to say yes and difficult to say no or to even have negative thoughts.

This is, of course, yet another occasion where your carefully crafted 'chip off the old block' student persona will provide you with assistance, because with this persona you will already appear to be the kind of person with whom academics can identify and want to assist. In your excuse, you may decide to underscore this persona by reminding them of your prodigious academic efforts this year, mentioning what you have achieved and intend to achieve, the importance of their course in achieving your scholarly objectives and the importance of their educational assistance. You may also mention how close you are to completion and point out precisely what you need to do and how much longer it will take to do it, thereby clearly demonstrating how your request for some extra time will be sufficient. In addition, your tone should be reasonable and sincere, while also being dignified yet respectful, using language that reflects a positive attitude and enthusiasm for your studies. If your educators already respect your academic ability they will be more accepting of excuses that are of a scholastic nature, such as regarding unforeseen obstacles to your research, like delayed access to a key source or the delay resulting from a need to redirect your research efforts after your first attempt did not produce the desired result. Less diligent students may have to rely on medical excuses with adequate documentation. The kind of excuses that you can give and their effectiveness will largely depend on how you are perceived. If a family crisis or medical problem has caused the delays, it will help your case if you inform your educator in advance that you may have difficulty meeting the submission date, rather than spring a request for an extension on your educator at the last minute. If they are briefed and updated regarding your concerns, they can often become sympathetically involved with your situation and this may encourage them to seek to do what they can to ease your predicament.

The increased prevalence of managerial values in university administration has led to an increased desire for productivity or successful student 'flow through', with departments wanting to produce a steady stream of graduates rather than drop-outs. This factor should work in your favour. So it may help your request to remind whomever is in authority over you that a little special consideration should produce an outcome that is desirable for all the parties concerned. Moreover, the introduction of university fees has also made a difference to the environment in which students may seek special consideration. The loss of a full-fee-paying student is a financial cost to a department that affects its financial viability and therefore its ability to employ its academics. If you are a full-fee-paying student, it is in the department's interests that you continue in the course, so it may be in your interest to tactfully remind them of your enrolment status, if you felt that a little extra persuasive muscle is required. But I remind you, many academics will be quite reasonable about granting modest extensions, so you may not have to play all your cards. Keep the aces up your sleeve for when you need them.

Making an unfamiliar environment familiar

Having covered your marshalling of the necessary material resources and support networks, the final dimension of your preparation to discuss is the need to acquaint yourself with an unfamiliar environment if you are starting at a new school or university. The confusion of being in an unfamiliar environment can hamper students' efforts to get their academic year off to a good start. If students are confused about directions and consequently arriving to lectures late and flustered, their psychological equilibrium will be upset and they will be less productive and less able to begin establishing the kind of keen, diligent, capable student persona that is in their interests to cultivate as soon as possible. To avoid this setback, familiarise yourself in advance with the public transport routes and their timetables or the driving routes and the nearby parking facilities. When you leave home, give yourself enough time to arrive early, so if you are delayed you will still arrive on time. Moreover, you should generally aim for an early arrival because it allows you to relax and tune into your environment before the lecture commences.

On your first day at a new school, you should take the initiative to use the recess time to determine the location of the classrooms and facilities that you will be using so you can promptly navigate from one to the other. If other students are confused, they can look to you for guidance. Those of you who are commencing university should allocate an afternoon before the first semester begins to explore its grounds and buildings. Unlike the cloistered environment of schools, universities are sprawling complexes, much like small towns. You will need to acquaint yourself with its main roads and pathways as well as determine the relevant buildings and locate your lecture halls and tutorial rooms so you can arrive on time to your classes. Next, you should determine the location of the faculty and departmental offices as well as their notice boards, along with the offices, telephone numbers and email addresses of your educators so you can consult them when necessary. You may also check out the campus facilities and shops, especially the academic book shops and their relevant stocks.

Most importantly, you need to acquaint yourself with the library, which will be the source of much of your learning. Fortunately, university libraries offer orientation tours at the commencement of the academic year, so promptly sign up for one, and then do so again at the beginning of each year to update your knowledge of this indispensable facility that is always changing, particularly under the impact of computerisation and the information revolution. You should also check the borrowing regulations and register for permission to borrow from libraries at other universities so you can swiftly avail yourself of this service when it is required. You should also determine whether there are specialist librarians who are relevant to your studies, noting their contact numbers so you can draw on their expertise when you commence your assignments. Finally, you should determine the location of the photocopy machines, the services of which you will have much need. In particular, see if there is a machine located in an obscure spot that few students know about, which you can resort to when the better known machines are all in use. These orientating measures are all intended to make you feel comfortable in your new environment so you can confidently focus on your performance from the commencement of your studies. After your initial orientation, you may choose to repeat a number of these necessary measures just before the beginning of each successive academic year.

Now that we have comprehensively dealt with the art of planning, preparing and marshalling your resources to establish the foundations for a successful year, it is appropriate to turn to mastering several of the specific academic skills that will bring greater success, namely learning, reading, note-taking, research and essay writing.

Becoming knowledgeable: The art of learning through reading and note-taking

You must approach the art of learning with the following reassuringly sensible principle in mind: **Knowledge builds in layers, with each layer facilitating the establishment of the next.** Students do not become experts overnight but they can become experts over longer time frames as their knowledge accumulates. It is also the case that the initial or early layers of knowledge are the most difficult to establish, especially in complex subjects, yet each layer of knowledge that you establish makes the next one easier to acquire. So, you should not be too hard on yourself if you initially experience some difficulty. Expect it. This is normal. Be patient but keep persevering. Although some new material will be easily understandable, there will be other times when you may not understand everything when you first encounter it. Be prepared to have further attempts at learning until understanding is soundly established. Your pace and depth of learning will largely depend on a combination of your natural ability and the number of layers of knowledge that you have established.

Preliminary or preparatory reading

With this in mind, it makes sense to establish the initial layers of knowledge as soon as possible to ensure that your overall learning experience is both easier and more productive. You do not even have to wait for the academic year to commence before you start your preparatory reading to lay down that first layer of knowledge. But where do you begin? For school students with clearly defined curricula involving a limited selection of textbooks (usually one per subject) this question is easy. Begin reading your prescribed textbooks early, shortly before the year commences and during the first weeks of the term when you can capitalise on the fact that the pace of work is much slower because the academic year has yet to build up a head of steam.

Take note that I have urged you to read the book, not to scrupulously study it. That will come later. Your purpose at this stage is to establish an initial layer of knowledge to make your note-taking in class more productive, your performance in class discussions more impressive, and to lay the groundwork for later successful attempts at acquiring a deeper understanding, as well as making your research for assessed assignments more confident, focused and effective. You should familiarise yourself with the material so you know what is covered, in what sequence it is presented, and where you can find various pieces of information. I remind you that I recommend that at this early stage you do not put yourself under pressure to fully understand all the material. Instead, allow this reading to be an enjoyable experience. Make yourself comfortable and then explore the material at a somewhat leisurely but still productive pace. It will be helpful if you underline significant passages in pencil or make some notes in the margins or jot down on a handy note pad some of your initial ideas, but keep in mind that at this stage these musings are exploratory rather than thorough. I remind you again that you are not yet engaged in research, that will come when you are working on an essay or preparing study notes for an exam response. You are merely becoming acquainted with the material.

Some of these textbooks, like comprehensive chronological narrative history texts, you should read from cover to cover to establish a broad sense of the overall 'story', including its major events and protagonists so you can later recognise them and appreciate their context when they are mentioned elsewhere. For texts that have chapters that can virtually stand alone, such as in psychology or biology, you may choose to skim read some chapters and concentrate on those that are more interesting or relevant to your studies.

Determining the most useful texts

For university students the task of selecting texts for preparatory reading requires astute judgement. At the commencement of your course, you will often be provided with a lecture and tutorial program, along with a list of essay questions and a reading guide that is relevant to the tutorial and essay topics. There may also be an accompanying booklet of photocopied readings. When many students first look at the reading guide for a university subject, they are often daunted by the large number of listed books and articles. Their first unnerving thought is often the impossibility of addressing all of them in the relatively short time frame of the course. Luckily, you do not have to do so. There is an art to making the most of a reading guide and it involves judicious selection. Firstly, university is unlike school in that you are being introduced in a more meaningful way to the wider world of organised knowledge and the reading guide represents a sample of the knowledge that is available in your subject. Rather than cover everything listed, you should consider your role to be to manoeuvre through this material, finding and capitalising upon the items that you will need and bypassing most of it. Some of you may come to appreciate these reading guides as formidable works of scholarship in their own right, being instructively organised so as to provide an orderly sense to a labyrinth of material that was otherwise incoherent. Despite the substantial instructive virtues of some of these guides, you should bear in mind that you are, of course, not restricted to the listed material and you can complement it with other sources as you see fit.

Scrutinise the reading guides in search of patterns, notably of a text or texts that are repeatedly mentioned as relevant to most tutorial topics. These are the ones you should read, preferably from cover to cover, as soon as possible, because these texts will provide you with the best possible orientation to the course and eventually provide basic subject matter for formulating essay and exam responses. It is usually advantageous to purchase these key texts so they will be readily accessible to you whenever you need them, which will be often. These few texts, sometimes as few as one in economics subjects like Business Management, can often provide you with the key to success for the whole course. But there may be potential pitfalls of which you must be aware. Firstly, a text may be repeatedly referred to as relevant to most topics principally because the lecturer wrote it. You may even notice a recommendation near the front of the reading guide strongly suggesting that you purchase this book. This is an ideal situation and great educational opportunity if your lecturer is the author of an authoritative textbook. This course can potentially provide you with some of your most rewarding educational experiences. Yet on the other hand, it is far less opportune to be hampered by a 'compulsory' text that is of limited educational value. You should be aware that academics often strike agreements with publishers by advising them of their captive audience so they can virtually guarantee the necessary minimum number of sales to close the publishing deal. While favourable references in your assignments to the lecturer's own work may be extremely advantageous in the pursuit of the highest grades, heavy reliance on a mediocre text may compromise your opportunity to maximise what you can learn while doing the course. Consequently, if you suspect that your lecturer's text is below a reasonable standard, check out the competition. Alternatives are usually found nearby on the library or bookshop shelf. You may decide to discreetly read a better quality text to enhance your learning while openly positively referring to the lecturer's text in your essay to maximise your grades.

Secondly, there may be some reading guides that do not readily reveal a pattern of frequently mentioned texts. For example, in some history subjects the recommended readings for each tutorial topic may focus on primary documents of specific rather than broad relevance, and worse, these documents may be unintelligible unless you already have a basic understanding of the subject. Lecturers who design their courses in this fashion may be doing what may seem to them to be appropriately 'scholarly' yet they are, unfortunately, falling a little short in their role as effective educators. You will need to compensate for these shortfalls by finding buried in the reading guide, or elsewhere, a general introductory text that encompasses the historical period and will therefore make this primary source material comprehensible. Many academics have become so comfortable with the fact that they possess substantial layers of detailed sophisticated knowledge that, unfortunately, they forget that the significance of these essential primary documents can only be appreciated in the context of the knowledge about the subject that they already have and take for granted that they have. Meanwhile their new students who are yet to acquire the knowledge necessary for that crucial sense of context are left bewildered until they take the initiative to read a general introductory text.

This principle may also hold if you find the booklet of prescribed readings to be too philosophically obscure or esoteric in nature. While many of these booklets of readings are well selected and well organised with items that are clearly introduced so they are easy to follow, other booklets can be somewhat alienating when first encountered. To avoid this dilemma, it will help you if you find and read a clearly written comprehensive introductory text before you read them, so that the significance of these documents becomes more appreciable. You will need to acquire your first layer of knowledge as soon as possible. Then when you read this photocopied booklet of material soon afterwards, it can in turn provide you with another layer of knowledge that is more detailed than the first.

So what are the benefits of this copious preparatory reading, which is done at a time when most students are still enjoying the more relaxed atmosphere of an academic year that does not yet seem to them to have properly commenced? Firstly, you should recognise that this preparatory reading is not adding extra to your workload. Instead, it will probably reduce it, or at least allow you to make the most productive use of your most precious and limited resource – time. There are very few corners to be cut in study if you are seeking the highest grades, but you can avoid most of the wild goose chases and wrong turns if you have a clearer idea of the nature of the subject before you commence your assignments.

Preparatory reading is analogous to carefully reading a map before you undertake a long journey into unfamiliar territory. The time spent reading a map often saves travelling time by allowing you to determine the most direct route to your destination. In a similar fashion, the preparatory reading lays the groundwork for more time efficient and effective research.

Preparatory reading also prevents procrastination by eliminating the bewilderment and fear of the unknown that can prevent many students from promptly getting started on their assignments. If you have done some preparatory reading, when you look at the list of assigned essay questions you will probably have ideas spring to mind on how you could answer several if not all the possible questions, or at least you will have a sense of where you could readily find material from which you could formulate answers. This is very reassuring. Meanwhile, other students will look at this list of questions and experience an unnerving sense of precarious vulnerability as they are confronted with the realisation that none of these questions make sense to them. Too many students become so unnerved by essay questions that they do not understand, as well as feel so intimidated by extensive reading lists, and become so alienated by incomprehensible documents in their prescribed reading booklet that they drop out of their course or university altogether. Preparatory reading can decisively boost a student's knowledge and morale to prevent this regrettable outcome.

Through preparatory reading, you can position yourself to concentrate on performing rather than merely surviving. Preparatory reading increases familiarity, and familiarity boosts confidence and confidence encourages action. If you are a year 12 high school student, think about how you would feel if you could pass year 12 by doing year 11 again; or, if you are a second year university student, think about what it would be like to be promoted to third year by doing your first year again. You would feel confident about the task because you are knowledgeable about what is involved and precisely what you need to do to succeed. Preparatory reading can help you to capture some of this winning attitude because your new subjects will become easier for you when you know something about them.

There are other benefits that preparatory reading can provide. University courses usually set weekly readings, with students expected to cover each relevant batch of material shortly in advance of attending their weekly tutorial. I recommend that you focus on preparatory reading in preference to weekly reading because weekly reading can sometimes lead to a misallocation of finite study time by distracting students during the semester from working on the assignments that produce grades. If your preparatory reading effectively covers the key introductory texts and examines the booklet of readings in the initial weeks following your commencement of the subject, you will be knowledgeable on virtually every tutorial topic well in advance, and therefore free to work virtually without distraction or interruption for the rest of the semester on the crucial assessed assignments and exam preparation. You are in a sense doing your weekly reading in advance, getting it over with so you can concentrate on more important matters. As a result, you will probably become more knowledgeable, and much sooner, than those students who simply routinely do the prescribed weekly reading on a weekly basis and you will probably perform as well or better than they do in class discussions. Weekly readings can sometimes become a pitfall that can compromise the success of otherwise capable students who fall into the trap of devoting too many hours to an activity that does not produce grades.

The benefits of an early start

As mentioned earlier, preparatory reading will eliminate the procrastination that is due to confusion over the comprehension of essay questions, thereby facilitating an early start on the assessed assignments that bring you valuable grades. **It requires almost the same degree of effort to get ahead and stay ahead as to keep up, so why not get ahead and benefit from the boost to your morale that being ahead brings.** Read through the essay questions, select your topic and start your assignment as soon as possible, ideally start as soon as you receive the questions and can determine the bias of your examiner that will affect how you will be assessed. This early start will make you feel like you are on top of the situation. It will maximise the time you have to plan and complete the project, allowing you to accommodate any setbacks or address any mistakes that could have been perilous if the project was commenced and executed at the last minute. It may also mean that you may be the first to borrow scarce library books.

While we are on the topic of early starts, in addition to an early start on an assignment, an early start on the day is also important. Have you ever noticed the television news programs broadcast very early in the morning, just before dawn? These programs serve the interests of the 'movers and shakers', such as businessman, politicians or academics who rise early and need to be briefed about the headlines or market trends at this opportune time as they prepare for their busy productive day ahead. Successful accomplished people are usually early risers. These people realise that if you begin the day early, you can maximise the number of hours when you can work effectively. So, if you find that you need a couple of extra hours to finish a task that day, they will be available, but not if you had started late. On the other hand, they also know that it is better to get up early to work solidly in the morning when they are fresh and more productive rather than to persevere late into the night when they will be tired and less able to concentrate. They understand that you can achieve more and in less time if you are fresh. Students can learn much from the habits of successful people. Rather than bide your time in the morning before your first lecture begins, you should complete several productive hours of study before you leave for university. It is better to use the tired evening hours to unwind and relax, treating this rest time as a reward for a hard day's work. Adherence to the principle of being an early riser and starting work early can dramatically improve your performance by adding productive hours to your efforts and allowing you to organise a more advantageous balance between work and relaxation. Nevertheless, it should be recognised that the body clocks of some people are wired to work better at night. While most people can adjust to rising early, these people should make the appropriate modifications to this principle to accommodate their predisposition.

Note-taking in class or lectures

As previously mentioned, preliminary reading can boost your performance regarding the art of note-taking in class or lectures by improving your comprehension of the material. Your preliminary reading often provides your first layer of knowledge while class or lecture notes usually provide the second, although sometimes this will be the other way around depending on the pace and content of your reading relative to the progress of the lecture program. In this fashion, these two sources of knowledge and processes of learning complement and reinforce each other. Your reading makes your understanding of the lectures more profound while your note-taking during the lectures makes your reading more effective.

Lectures can be highly informative and sometimes entertaining as well. They are most helpful when they provide you with a concise insightful interesting account of a topic that serves as a useful orientation, but they have their limitations. They are not a substitute, as some students assume, for the reading and research that is required to produce essays that achieve high grades yet, on the other hand, they can assist this reading and research.

Lectures can be an excellent way to learn, but you should recognise that the benefits of a good lecture are quickly lost unless you take notes, and the more notes that you take the greater the benefits will be. With this in mind, university students should maximise the benefits gained from note-taking by taking them in tutorials as well, something that many neglect to do. Some tutorials are very informative, especially when a talented tutor transforms the event into an interactive mini-lecture where you can ask questions. Take notes even when the tutorial is mostly consumed by a tutorial paper delivered by a fellow student because there may be material that is of value for you to record. If you are in doubt about the value of what is said, take notes anyway.

Because this note-taking is important, I advise university students to try to attend all their lectures and tutorials and school students to attend their scheduled classes. There are other benefits for you in addition to the notes that you can take. Regular attendance helps to instil in you a valuable sense of discipline and reinforce your commitment to your objective in a fashion that will positively carry over into the attitude in which you complete your assignments. Even when you believe that the quality of the lectures or lessons is disappointing, still attend them. Only skip lectures, tutorials or classes if you have pressing due dates for assessed assignments or exam preparation that cannot be completed without such measures. You will need to weigh up the difference between the cost of missing the classes and the benefits stemming from the time reallocated to completing assessed work. What pays in grades should always take priority. In this context, time taken off school or university in the pursuit of leisure should be avoided or minimised because it encourages attitudes that are not conducive to success. What can become a major problem usually begins in a seemingly harmless fashion and develops into self-sabotage before the student realises what has happened.

Regular attendance is also essential if you are to establish an appropriate student persona, that of the keen, diligent, capable student or the 'chip off the old block', which will positively affect how you are perceived and treated by your examiners. In addition, your attendance may possibly be appreciated even more if your educator is less competent and their feelings have been hurt by the resulting high absenteeism. The more students who do not attend, the more your attendance will be noticed and appreciated as a vote of confidence. If you make the lecturer feel more positive about himself, he will feel more positively disposed towards you and consequently assess your assignments with a more favourable attitude. The lecturer may also exclusively share with those few in attendance some valuable clues about how to succeed in the exam as a reward for their appearance of loyalty. In addition, be alert to the possibility that if a teacher or lecturer is hurriedly trying to cram a great deal of material into the final few classes or lectures, this is usually a clue that this material will feature in the exam, and the teacher or lecturer is worried about being caught falling short in his duties, so treat this last minute material as valuable in your exam preparations. Furthermore, as discussed extensively in the second chapter of this book, you should also use your lectures, tutorials or classes as opportunities to record information that will allow you to construct a psychological profile of your examiner, information that will give you a clear understanding of precisely what you have to do to achieve high grades.

I have previously described the process of note-taking in classes or lectures in the second chapter of this book, yet to make this chapter on fundamental study skills more helpful, some points about the procedure require additional detailed discussion. To take notes effectively you should arrive early. In your lecture pad that is designated for the subject you can note at the top of your first page the date and topic. You should also mention the time, especially if you are attending one of a choice of alternative lecture times (usually either morning or evening), and note the lecturer's name, especially if it is a guest lecturer. You may also mention the venue, such as the university building and lecture hall. As you may have noticed, this is more identifying detail than required for note-taking in high school classes. It means that you have recorded the identifying details about the lecture in a scholarly fashion that will allow you to possibly make reference to it in a footnote or bibliography, just in the rare case that this later becomes necessary. It should be noted that generally lecturers frown on footnotes in students' essays to their lectures, perceiving this as evidence of a lack of reading, yet if the content of the lecture was original they would in this circumstance appreciate your diligence. Next, you can number several pages in your lecture pad to save time later while you are vigorously taking notes. You are now ready to write.

As I advised you in the second chapter of this book, take notes in full sentences as much as possible rather than in point form. The danger of taking notes in point form is that students often abbreviate the material so severely that they unintentionally distort its meaning. This may not seem to be the case at the time because the information is fresh and students can still recall much of the rest of the spoken information that makes these abbreviated points intelligible. Yet when students attempt to read this material in three or six months time while researching an essay or preparing for exams, it is disappointingly discovered to be mostly incomprehensible and of far less value than anticipated. When students take abbreviated notes in this fashion, they are in effect relying on two sets of notes, one set being incompletely recorded on the page and the other retained imperfectly in the memory. The situation is analogous to a treasure map that is torn in two with each half being useless without the other. The danger stems from the way that the half of the treasure map that is represented by the material recorded in the memory fades rapidly, leaving the half that is recorded in points in the lecture pad to eventually be far less helpful than intended. However, if you try to write down as much as possible in full sentences then what you do record will be understandable and useful when you need it. Moreover, the notes will read better, thereby making more of an impression on you as you study them, and because of this, you will appreciate them more. Meanwhile, those unfortunate students who do not take notes in this fashion usually find themselves left with a confusing array of half-recorded ideas to study. While reading these notes they will experience the frustration of frequently having to pause to try to figure out what the notes mean, and this can become very disorienting, virtually defeating one of the purposes of notes to provide convenient access to the material in the lectures.

In the pursuit of clarity and ease of use, you should also use plenty of sub-headings to identify the content of the material at a glance. You may also choose to underline comments that were particularly important. In addition, it will help if you draw a box around any recommendations regarding important texts that may help you in your studies or asterisk any valuable tips about the nature of the exams or the assessment of essays. Furthermore, to benefit fully from note-taking you should also have the attitude that once the lecture has finished your note-taking has finished. This process, important as it is, should not intrude on any more of your valuable time than is necessary. You should appreciate that this process is primarily a means to an end rather than an end in itself. By adopting this method of note-taking you will find that, although you will not manage to record everything, you will record a great deal of useful information and your effectiveness will improve even more with practice.

Before we move on to discuss the different methods of reading and note-taking used for research purposes, there are a couple more points to appreciate about note-taking in classes or lectures. Even though some lectures are conducted in power point presentations, which can often include printed handouts covering the points seen in the overhead display, you should still take additional notes and not use this printed material as an excuse to sit back and relax. As the treasure map analogy implies, it is the additional verbally communicated explanations that usually bring the abbreviated points to life and make their meanings more apparent. You may find it profitable to record as much of the spoken material as you can by writing directly on the handouts to flesh out the implications of the listed points, or you may take notes in your lecture pad as you normally would, filing the printed handout with them to serve as a supplement.

Furthermore, it is generally more profitable to take written notes rather than record lectures on audiotape. If you do tape record, do so in addition to diligent note-taking rather than as an alternative to it. Furthermore, you should ensure that the tapes are clearly labelled so their contents are obvious and not accidentally erased. Generally, you should only tape-record a lecture if you are seeking to preserve it as a special event, perhaps because of the appearance of a talented guest lecturer or because important material relevant to your central interests will be covered in detail. The danger involved in relying on regularly taping lectures stems largely from how the laborious time-consuming process of transcribing them can add so much to your workload that you may have little time left to do the assignments that deliver grades. Just as with the spending of too much time on weekly tutorial readings, this misallocation of precious time can lead to otherwise capable students achieving results far less than their potential, despite their efforts.

Becoming effective: The art of reading and note-taking for research

Learning is important but the majority of your time should be devoted to using the study skills that directly put points on the board in terms of grades. There are different modes of reading and note-taking for different purposes and you will need to be able to employ each of them. Most people can read but few people can read like an academic. This is similar to the fact that most people can run but few people can run like an athlete. Just as there are different techniques for running sprints or long distances there are different modes of reading for different purposes. We have discussed preparatory reading, which is exploratory reading, now we turn to the art of reading for research, which is purposeful reading. Even though this reading will also add substantial additional layers to your knowledge, treat this benefit as an incidental bonus because the principal purpose of this reading is to produce the notes from which essays or exam responses may be written.

Selecting topics for study

However, before you can commence your research, you need to pick a topic from the alternatives on the list of essay questions. Having done some preparatory reading, some diligent note-taking in class and perhaps already possessing some relevant general knowledge, this will make your task easier, so will the information provided by the psychological profile of your examiner that you compiled, in particular your appreciation of their bias and their understanding of the subject. The criteria that you use to select a topic will be determined by your objectives. If your aim is maximise your understanding of the core subject matter of the course, then pick a topic that seems to be of central relevance, so your research will greatly enhance your overall grasp of the subject. If your prime interest is an aspect of the subject that interests you and inspires your enthusiasm, with this interest perhaps being the main reason why you enrolled, then seize the opportunity to pursue this curiosity further via your research. Some students may pick a topic for practical reasons, either because it was one of the few questions that made sense or because they believe that more resources such as library books are available for that topic. For those students who seek the highest grades, I advise you that picking the topic constitutes a substantial part of the effort. Pick topics that are in tune with the bias of your examiner to allow you to fully capitalise on it. Ideally, try to select a topic in which you also have a genuine interest or, even better, share the bias of your examiner (if that is possible) so you can pursue your research with greater enthusiasm.

In addition to your examiner's bias, you can choose topics to allow you to exploit the strengths or weaknesses of their knowledge of the subject, following the principles discussed in the second chapter of the book as the analogy of the 'black shoe'. An academic may know a great deal about a subject but no matter how expert they are there will still be gaps in their knowledge that are usually covered over by bluff or avoidance or by an honest acknowledgement of their limitations. In your bid for high grades, you can choose topics to capitalise either on their wisdom or on the gaps in their wisdom. For example, a university subject covering the history of the French Revolution usually begins with a study of the Ancien Régime then progresses through the phases of the Revolution to cover Napoleonic France before it concludes with the restoration of the Bourbon monarchy. If a lecturer in this subject has researched the Ancien Régime in depth but has read comparatively little about Napoleonic France, students can expect that he will know a great deal about the Ancien Régime and have a comparatively basic understanding of Napoleonic France. If a student chose to write an essay on the Ancien Régime then it is inevitable that this examiner will be aware of about 20 or more relevant points that the student could have also considered or 50 or more references that could have been consulted. This academic's considerable knowledge on this topic will enable him to be more aware of the limitations of a student's work, no matter how accomplished it may be for an undergraduate. By choosing topics in areas where the examiner is most knowledgeable, students can risk coming under an unfairly high level of scrutiny, usually without the examiner being aware that he has this inclination towards being tougher on those students who may share his enthusiasms and follow in his footsteps.

It is possible that the examiner's formidable wisdom will work against students scoring the highest grades on this topic unless they play a little smarter. If you do choose to write on the topic in which your examiner is particularly expert, it is advised that you closely mirror the examiner's appreciation of the significant scholarship in this area or, better still, look up the examiner's own publications on the topic and extol their value in your essay. Alternatively, if a student chooses to write on the topic about which the examiner knows less, in this case Napoleonic France, and then writes well, it is likely that this student may be adding to the examiner's knowledge about the topic, or at least be providing him with a useful revision of the basic material. Some examiners may handsomely reward students for this service. In addition, because the examiner's knowledge is limited, he may not be aware of many of the other texts the student could have consulted, while some minor problems or limitations in the student's work may go unnoticed and unpenalised.

Understanding the three types of essay questions

Having chosen a topic, the next step in your research is to address the question to determine what it requires of you, a process that will in turn provide you with your initial clues to help you to decide what to read and what to read first. This is because research involves reading with a specific question in mind. Moreover, because the nature of the question influences the nature of your research, it is opportune at this point to learn more about the nature of essay questions before we closely examine the research process. This analysis of the nature of essay questions is also intended to demystify them for you so you are not unsettled by them and instead feel more comfortable and confident about addressing them. This wisdom is to help you to become in tune with the following empowering principle.

Do not let the question intimidate you. Instead, you should intimidate the question. We shall return to the important topic of addressing questions when we look at it later in the context of the art of essay writing.

To make this analysis of the nature of essay questions easier for you to appreciate, I have used examples that I encountered when helping year 12 English students deal with assignment and exam questions regarding William Shakespeare's famous play *Othello*. So you can better appreciate my analysis of these questions, it will help if I initially provide you with a concise account of the key themes or meaning of Shakespeare's play.

Shakespeare's *Othello* is one of his greatest and most psychologically insightful tragedies. True to the genre of the tragedy, the play tells the story of how a great man, in this case Othello, who is a Moorish mercenary general in the pay of the Venetian government, is brought down by a fatal flaw in his character, in this case jealousy. The audience, having initially been encouraged to appreciate and admire Othello's noble qualities, and his profound love for his new wife Desdemona, is by the end of the play confronted by Othello's murder of his wife, who dies shortly before Othello learns that she was innocent of the infidelity that he suspected, a revelation followed closely by his self-inflicted punishment of suicide. Consequently, the play encourages the audience to reflect upon the dangers of jealousy as a fatal flaw and how they could avoid succumbing to it themselves. Secondly, the play is about deception and misperception, revealing how an intelligent honourable man like Othello can be fooled, and be encouraged to fool himself, as he is caught in the web of deception spun by the sociopathic Iago, a Venetian officer who sought revenge on Othello and another officer, Cassio, because Othello promoted Cassio ahead of him. Iago's evil machinations fuel Othello's jealousy and help drive the plot until his ambitious schemes come undone, leaving Iago and his principled wife Emilia, who discovered and revealed her husband's treachery, among the fatalities of the final Act. A sub-theme of great interest to anti-racist politically correct educators is the issue of racial difference. Othello is black, and although trusted and honoured by the Venetian court, he is not fully accepted in white Venetian society. This is evident when Brabantio who had wholeheartedly accepted Othello as an esteemed houseguest later reluctantly accepted him as a son-in-law when this union with his daughter Desdemona was a fait accompli. Meanwhile, Othello's internalised sense of 'otherness' added to his insecure fears that his Venetian wife could be tempted by Cassio, who is a handsome member of her own kind, as Iago deceitfully suggested to him. Now that you understand the meaning of this play, we can return to our analysis of the nature of essay questions.

When addressing an essay question for an assignment or an exam it helps to appreciate that there are only three types of questions that you can be asked. The first type of essay questions are intelligent questions conceived by intelligent educators that seem to go to the heart of the topic or issue or debate, or relate directly to the key theme of the text being studied; or they focus on a clearly identifiable aspect of a topic or issue or debate, or on a sub-theme of a text. These are questions written by educators who understand their subject and know how to phrase a question. When you research these questions, you will notice that they seem to require you to acquire and express knowledge that is central to the meaning of the topic or relevant to a clearly recognisable significant aspect of the topic. To most students undertaking research, these questions are more likely to seem to make sense to them and be appreciated as worthy of investigation. Moreover, you are more likely to find greater amounts of relevant information and analysis in the literature when investigating these kinds of questions. These are the ideal assignment or exam questions to choose if you have to select from options.

An example of this kind of question would be:

'*Othello* is much more a story of jealousy than of love.' Discuss.

This well-conceived but nevertheless quite demanding question invites students to draw attention to the focus of the play on an aspect of love, jealousy, rather than the broader subject of love itself, which would then lead into a discussion of the principal theme of the play regarding jealousy as Othello's fatal flaw. Alternatively, some students may focus their response more broadly to argue that the secondary or sub-themes are sufficiently connected to Othello's jealousy to allow these elements to be discussed along with the principal theme.

The second type of essay questions are those that are consciously designed to be different to last year's question on the same topic,

or different to the other questions on a list of options. They can seem like sensible questions that have been given a deliberate twist, or like ones that deliberately focus on a less obvious aspect of the topic. They are written by educators who believe that questions should not repeat themselves from year to year, or by educators who had to produce a long list of questions on the same topic but after a point began to run short of ideas. As a result, at first glance they can sometimes seem novel and throw students a little off balance until calm reflection reveals that these questions are relevant to the main or other significant concerns of the topic, only they focus on less obvious dimensions or look at the topic from a different angle. The research required to deal with this type of question should seek information and analysis covering the main or significant concerns of the topic while also paying attention to the distinctive dimension or angle highlighted by the question. If you focus solely on gathering information and analysis on the novel aspect of the question while researching it, you may find that your understanding of the topic will be improperly anchored and probably drift off course to produce patchy or confusingly specific notes. The resulting difficulty in understanding the topic will usually produce difficulty in effectively answering the question. Nevertheless, you can avoid that danger by taking some notes that are of a more general or comprehensive nature than the question seemed to require. It is later when drafting your response to this type of question that you need to sharpen your focus on the terms of the question to ensure the precise relevance of your answer.

An example of this type of question is the following:

'Desdemona suffers the most tragic fate of all characters in the play.' Do you agree?

This is a question with a deliberate twist that revolves around its employment of the common understanding of the meaning of the term tragedy (an unfortunate event usually where someone dies) instead of the meaning of the term in literature (where a great man or hero falls from grace due to a flaw in his character), and in doing so shifts attention from Othello to his unfortunate wife. Students would be expected to juxtapose the competing concepts of tragedy and their implications in a comparison of the 'tragic fates' of characters, such as Othello and Desdemona, or to resolutely assert the dominance of the literary definition of tragedy in this play and thereby refocus the question back on Othello to discuss Desdemona's fate in terms of her role in Othello's tragedy.

The third type of essay questions are those that are written by educators who either do not know their subject well or how to intelligently phrase a question. This type should not to be confused with questions that deliberately include statements that are incorrect to stimulate students to offer a correction in their answer. Instead, these questions are noticeably more strange. At their worst, they are confrontingly baffling due to their apparent irrationality or because their relevance to the major or minor concerns of the topic is tenuous at best. Sometimes, these kinds of questions can be produced by teachers or academics who may know the subject quite well but are poor educators, consequently they produce questions that are oblique or obscure, often reflecting the examiner's ideologically driven or esoteric pet curiosities and consequently being of marginal importance and of doubtful value as an avenue for research. On other occasions, these questions are written by reasonably competent educators who produced other good questions but later ran out of ideas, for example when being expected to produce a list of twelve questions but they could only think of eight sensible ones, with the last four being desperate concoctions produced solely to fill the quota. It is strongly recommended that if you suspect that you have been presented with options of this nature, you should avoid them in favour of other choices.

When researching this type of question, students may find it difficult to find relevant texts or materials from which to formulate an answer. Worse, these questions can lead students off track and confuse their understanding of the topic. In exams, students may not have the option to avoid this type of question, but do not despair, there are methods for turning these exam questions into first-rate performances. If unfortunately you cannot avoid this type of question as an assigned essay question, the way to handle it profitably is similar to the way you would treat it in an exam. You recontextualise the question. You would, in a scholarly fashion, redefine the question, then research and respond to its specific demands in the context of a more relevant theme or argument or issue or dimension of the topic, responding as you would as if responding to the redefined question was what you were originally asked to do. Later, in the introduction to your essay, you would tactfully justify your approach by stating something like the following:

> Although the author does touch upon the point [referred to in the question] several times in his novel, his principal concern was in expressing [his main theme] and he only touched upon this point in this context. This essay shall examine this point in the context of [this main theme] because it is in this context that this point can be best appreciated.

Remember that it will help if you adopt a polite, respectful tone as you redefine the question, to avoid any chance of offending your examiner or making them feel that you have strayed from the topic, which you have not done.

This type of question can be illustrated by the following example:

> '*Othello* is a racist play both in the way characters deceive and treat Othello and how Othello ultimately envisages himself.' Discuss.

This clumsily worded question reflects the fascination with anti-racism of the educator who wrote the question (which, by the way, would be shared by many other teachers) more so than it tunes into Shakespeare's principal concerns. The misleading terminology 'racist play' implies either that the play is significantly about racism or that it espouses racist beliefs. Despite this shortcoming, the question does accurately refer to the principal dimensions of the sub-theme of racial difference touched upon in the play (namely the Venetians' perceptions of Othello and his perception of himself), allowing the student to tactfully redefine the question in terms of this sub-theme before discussing it.

Now that we have critically categorised questions in a manner that can help you to select from and respond to different types of questions, it will also help you if we look at some of the different ways that questions are presented. To help you to appreciate this analysis of the way questions are expressed, it will help if I remind you of the purpose of essay questions. They are intended to precipitate relevant essay responses from students on a particular topic, an essay being an argument consisting of a contention that is logically supported by reason and evidence arranged sequentially in successive paragraphs.

You would have noticed that essay questions can be expressed in a number of different ways. Some questions include a quote from a text followed by a relevant question to which students must respond. For example:

> In *Othello*, love is destroyed by jealousy, the 'green-eyed monster, which doth mock / The meat it feeds on' (III. 3). Does the text support this view?

Be aware that usually, but not always, the key to the meaning of a question expressed in this form is not found in the words of the quotation, which usually provides additional illustration or clarification, as it does in this case, but in the other phrases in the question, especially the final part that actually asks something of the students, as the second sentence in this question does. In this example, students are expected to argue that the play provides ample evidence for its central theme of how Othello's jealousy destroyed his marriage and in doing so, destroyed him.

In addition, students should watch out for essay questions that include statements in quotation marks that are followed by the terms 'Do you agree' or 'Discuss' that seem to masquerade as scholarly opinion to which the student must respond. This form of presentation was evident in several of the questions discussed earlier:

> '*Othello* is much more a story of jealousy than of love.' Discuss.
>
> 'Desdemona suffers the most tragic fate of all characters in the play.' Do you agree?

These quotation marks can sometimes intimidate some students who may feel compelled to agree with the statement enclosed in them because they fear that it may be authoritative. It may reassure you to know that these statements were probably written by teachers (acting in the role of examiners) and their presentation in quotation marks is merely stylistic, so feel free to critically engage with the statement in the question if you feel that is necessary, as it would be with the second question in the above examples. Indeed, with some deliberately tricky questions expressed in this manner, the high performing students will be expected by their examiner to contend with the assumptions inherent in the statement enclosed in quotation marks.

Furthermore, despite the fuss to the contrary made by some teachers, the terms 'Do you agree' or 'Discuss' amount to the same thing in the practice of writing a response to an essay question. Rather than being 'key terms' representing profoundly different kinds of questions, they are simply linguistic devices added to the end of a statement in order to turn it into a question that requires an essay response. This similarity becomes evident when you think carefully about what each of these terms requires. Any expression of agreement or disagreement will entail a discussion of the topic as you support your contention with reason and evidence. Similarly, if you discuss the topic in the context of presenting an argument on it you will usually at some stage express or imply some degree of agreement or disagreement with it. So what's the difference in practice? There may be more important terms in an essay question to take into consideration than 'Do you agree' or 'Discuss', such as 'who' and 'what', or 'how' and 'why', or 'where' and 'when', with terms like 'how' or 'why' inviting a more theoretical answer than the more factual requests involving 'where' or 'when'.

When interpreting some questions, students need to pay attention to methodological cues, such as the use of feminist or other forms of theoretical terminology. These cues are often more important indicators of the examiner's expectations than the apparent topic of the question because they point out to students the kind of analysis they are expected to undertake, including the kind of evidence they are expected to identify and discuss in the primary sources, and the kind of academic opinion they are expected to find and draw upon. One of these cues can be found in the following question:

> '*Othello* is a shattering case study in male victimisation of women.' Discuss.

Shakespeare's *Othello* centres on male characters. He did not set out to write a play about the subject implied by this question. Nevertheless, the setting for this drama does depict a patriarchal society that subordinates women and Shakespeare's characterisation of female characters in this society can be explored from a feminist perspective that looks at the play in terms of what it may reveal about the dominant social values of Shakespeare's era. This would be the angle or methodological approach that students would be expected to take when responding to this question.

Students should also watch out for terms that indicate the ideological bias of the examiner, such as the use of value-laden words that seem intended to colour the readers' response to the subject matter by expressing some sense of approval or disapproval or favour or disfavour. For example, a question might refer to a government policy as 'progressive', thereby suggesting approval, or label a conservative politician as 'reactionary', thereby suggesting disfavour. In the feminist question on Shakespeare's *Othello* mentioned above, the terminology 'male victimisation of women' is value-laden, implying disapproval of the gender hierarchy and the treatment of the female characters by the male characters depicted in the play. This value-laden terminology could be interpreted as revealing the examiner's favoured ideology, values and ethics. Because of the significant impact that bias can have on assessment, it would be in students' interests to reflect the bias detected in the wording of the question in their answers.

Students should also watch out for questions that may require them to focus on a particular form of material to support their answers. The material that you are expected to draw upon in your research can be divided into two broad categories. The first is primary sources such as historical documents, the actual novel or play or painting, etc., that is being studied, or sociological survey data. The second kind of material is found in secondary sources that are understood to be for the most part organised in 'debates' among academics and other protagonists, with these debates being assumed to be conducted primarily through printed publications rather than the spoken word. If the question specifically asks students to, for example, discuss a play by drawing on evidence from the text, this does not mean that students should interpret the question as requiring them to skip any consultation of secondary sources that examine the text. Instead, these sources should be sought by students to provide them with valuable clues as to what evidence to highlight in their analysis. This emphasis on using primary evidence is evident in one of the questions on *Othello* that we discussed earlier:

> In *Othello*, love is destroyed by jealousy, the 'green-eyed monster, which doth mock / The meat it feeds on' (III. 3). Does the text support this view?

Although they may have researched a number of secondary sources in addition to a close examination of the text, students answering this question in an essay should ensure that they primarily supported their arguments with evidence drawn directly from the play.

Another form of question that is more likely to be asked of university rather than high school students involves requesting students to critically evaluate a theory or interpretation of a topic. Essay responses would involve firstly clearly and succinctly defining that theory or interpretation so that the analysis proceeds from a solid foundation. It would then involve one or more of the following processes: a critical assessment of significant academic and other commentary on this theory or interpretation, or an assessment of the implications for this theory or interpretation arising from other relevant scholarship on the topic even though this scholarship may not directly address the theory or interpretation being examined, or the use of primary sources to test the value or credibility of the theory or interpretation, or a critical look at the implications of this theory or interpretation for other scholarship in this area. That is how students should respond to this typical example of this form of question that I found while exploring tertiary English courses on the internet. The question is related to an interpretation of *Othello* that argued that the shift during the play of the setting, from civilised Venice to Cyprus, which is seen as a frontier post at the edge of civilisation, was a key ingredient for the explosion of passions that brought the story to a climax:

> Respond to Alvin Kernan's essay, 'Barbarism and the City'. What is Kernan's thesis? Does it hold up for *Othello*? Where do you agree with his essay, and why? Where do you disagree, and what in the text of the play leads you to disagree?

Research

Having learnt more about judicious topic selection and interpreting the nature of essay questions, we can return to the art of reading and note-taking for research, an important endeavour that will take up a great deal of your productive time as a student. There are three phases to the researching and writing of an essay, or to researching and producing notes to study for exams. The first phase involves a purposeful form of exploratory reading intended to find, identify and rate potential sources as most helpful or less helpful, while the unhelpful sources are weeded out and dismissed. The second phase involves extracting the notes from which the essay will be written or from which the exam study notes will be produced. The few most helpful sources are subjected to detailed systematic note-taking, while the sources designated as less helpful are the subject of less detailed note-taking to produce additional material that complements the notes taken from the most important sources. The third phase involves drafting and editing an essay. If you are producing study notes for exams, it involves synthesising the extracted notes, along with your lecture notes and any other relevant material, so they tell one story. The synthesised material should also ideally be of a length that allows you to study it effectively within the time you have available for learning within the 24 hour period preceding the exam.

Exploratory reading

Your assessment of the nature and demands of the essay question will have provided you with some initial clues about what you need to do for your research, yet it is this process of purposeful exploratory reading that will contribute most to solving the perplexing problem for many students of where to start, and in determining where to take detailed notes and where to take brief notes. The selection and rating of sources according to their utility is a vital skill because the production of assigned essays and exam preparation is done against the clock. High school and undergraduate students do not have the time to thoroughly read and take notes from more than a few texts, so the research process should begin by gathering a substantial amount of relevant material, inspecting it, rating it, then organising these potential sources in a hierarchy of importance. What you are looking for is the one, two, three or perhaps four key texts that will be the most useful to you (the fewer the better), which will be the focus of most of your note-taking to derive the bulk of the material from which you will formulate and express your answer, or produce perceptive and comprehensive exam study notes. The process of research is the same for high school and undergraduate students, although undergraduates are expected to demonstrate that they have conducted their research more thoroughly by consulting more references. Some of you may be thinking that my advice about gathering sources in order to narrow the note-taking down to a few texts goes against the need to demonstrate the kind of wide reading and to show the lengthy bibliography in your essay that most examiners like to reward. Do not worry. These additional texts will be factored in later. To even think about note-taking from many texts at this early stage is to invite confusion.

You begin the research process by listing then gathering relevant sources. Your preparatory reading for the course should have provided you with some initial ideas as to what texts to assemble although your greatest source of assistance should come from the course reading guide. In addition, you may have noted some tips regarding valuable texts during lectures or tutorials, or been informed about useful materials by chatting to your educators or classmates about your assignment, all of which can be added to your list of potential sources.

At this stage, you are interested in maximising the amount of sources you can gather before you winnow it down to the essential few. If the reading guide has listed, for example, five or ten or as many as twenty titles as relevant to the topic, try and locate all of them so you can check each of them and therefore maximise your choice. As you look up the library call numbers, either in the library or at home on your computer, you may also take the opportunity to read the synopses of various texts on the library's data base, which may provide some helpful initial clues as to their usefulness. In addition, you may discover other titles listed near the specific text that you were looking for that seem potentially useful that you can add to your list. After you have determined the library call numbers, find yourself a quiet private place in the library where you can pile the potential sources for inspection, then begin your hunt. As you collect the books and journal articles, check the titles on the shelves nearby. The library system stores materials firstly by subject and then alphabetically by author, so this means that you may come across other potentially useful references that may have been overlooked by the reading guide. Gather those as well. **A good researcher needs to be focused on the task but at the same time aware that valuable sources may appear by chance in their peripheral vision. A good researcher needs to be open to the possibility that they may come across some valuable material by accident.** That is why you initially cast your net widely.

Even though I am stressing the value of gathering a quantity of material at this early stage in the research process, you also need to make sure that you locate those sources that are essential to complete the task, such as the text that presents the theory or data that you have to critically evaluate or one that is particularly insightful or one that reviews the literature on the topic thereby providing valuable summaries of the major contributions to the relevant academic debate. **You should hunt for these vital sources with the determined attitude that you will not take no for an answer regarding their availability. It is this hunger to do what you know you need to do no matter what obstacles may be in your path that distinguishes a good researcher.** If you are a high school student and the book that you seek is not available at your school library, go to a university library that is far better resourced. If you are a tertiary student and the book that you require is not available on the shelves at your university library, go to the reserve desk that holds the texts in high demand, rationing them for two hour loans; then when it is your turn to borrow it, use the photocopier to gather the material you need. If this is not possible, try borrowing the book from another library. If it is not in another library in your town, inquire as to whether a copy can be sent to you from another library interstate, although there may be a delay due to postage. Alternatively, ask a lecturer or tutor to lend you a copy, or see if you can borrow the book from a well-resourced classmate. On the other hand, you could buy the book at an academic bookstore or if that is not possible, purchase it via the internet, although, as with interstate loans, this process takes longer due to postage. Do not let the lack of a key text provide you with an excuse to do nothing. **While engaged in research, treat each obstacle as a mere setback, a new challenge to be overcome.** Only if you have exhausted these options should you consider briefly postponing the project, busying yourself in the meantime with other studies until the situation improves.

Selecting the most useful sources

When you have established a pile of all the relevant potentially useful texts, it is time to sort the wheat from the chaff, to rate the sources as to their value regarding your project. To do this you have to employ the valuable reading skill of acquainting yourself with a text. The first item to look at is the title. Is it relevant? Titles can provide a major clue as to what a book is about but sometimes they are vague or misleading. For example, *The Whitlam Government: 1972-1975*, by the former Australian Labor Party Prime Minister Gough Whitlam and *A Certain Grandeur* by Graham Freudenberg (who had been Whitlam's press secretary, principal speech writer and political adviser) are both about the political career of Gough Whitlam, but only one of these books makes it clear in the title that is printed on the spine of the book. Consequently, *A Certain Grandeur* could easily be overlooked by students searching the shelves for relevant sources when researching the Whitlam Government. In some cases, the subtitles of books often provide a better indication as to its contents than the main title. If one pulled the Freudenberg book off the shelf and looked at its front cover or its title page near the front of the book, one would notice the book's more informative full title (which is the combined main title and subtitle), *A Certain Grandeur: Gough Whitlam in Politics*, which gives a clearer indication of its potential usefulness.

The year of publication, indicated near the front of the book, is also important because it provides clues as to the context in which the book was written, which was before and up to the year of publication, and the context in which it emerged into the public arena, which was at or soon after that date. For example, Freudenberg's book was published in 1977, the year that Gough Whitlam retired from parliamentary politics, so it was a relatively fresh account when it first appeared. Nevertheless, the benefits of this timeliness reduce over time, and subsequent students may see this date of publication as suggesting that the author did not spend time to thoroughly research and carefully reflect on many of the events that the book describes. Meanwhile, Whitlam's memoir and historical account was published in 1985, indicating the possibility that more time was spent researching and reflecting on the nature of the events that the book covers. This may be a clue that Whitlam's book may be a more opportune place to start note-taking than Freudenberg's book, which could be treated as a less important source to supplement the information derived from *The Whitlam Government: 1972-1975*.

When acquainting themselves with a text, students should also attempt to assess the nature of the author, which will provide clues as to the perspective the book takes on the topics it covers. Helpful information in this regard can be found in the brief biographical details about the author that are usually found on the back of the book or on the inside flap of the book's dust cover. In the examples of Whitlam and Freudenberg mentioned above, neither of the authors were academics and both were involved in many of the political events that they described, so their accounts could be expected to be informative yet also highly subjective and sympathetic towards a controversial government that polarised national opinion. Edited collections that feature many specialist authors, usually with each one having written different chapters on different topics, often provide brief biographical details of the authors at the front of the book to allow you to check their principal academic interests, appointments that they hold or have held, and their former publications, all of which can give clues to students as to these authors' expertise and biases. For example, the collection edited by the academics Christine Jennet and Randal G. Stewart, *Hawke and Australian Public Policy: Consensus and Restructuring*, includes chapters covering developments in each major area of public policy while Bob Hawke was the Labor Prime Minister. When checking the authors' biographical details, students may notice that a significant number of the contributing academics had expertise in areas like race, class, gender, and peace research, which can be interpreted as suggesting that the chapters written by these people may reflect politically correct Left values. Meanwhile, the chapter written by an academic who had previously written on more traditional public policy topics, and published a case study of the Liberal Prime Minister Malcolm Fraser, could possibly be expected to have looked at the subject matter from a different perspective.

If you are studying an area that is relatively new to you, the names of the authors may initially mean little as you read about them. You should persevere, because this kind of intelligence gathering will give you a keener understanding of the nature of the literature with which you will be working. Your bewilderment will pass with the more research that you do. The more familiar you become with the academics and other authors in the area, the more adept you will become at classifying where they fit into the debate. Not only does understanding the nature of the authors give you clues as to the contents of their books, it will give you the ability to critically assess and write about these authors' contributions to the debate in a more scholarly manner, which is something more like the approach of the academics who will be assessing you, most of whom are very familiar with this kind of information. While on the topic of seeking a greater understanding of authors, the book's preface or acknowledgements can provide students with useful clues as to the academic or other networks in which an author may be involved, and this information can help you to classify them as belonging to a school of thought or ideological camp. Some authors may pay homage to a leading academic or key thinker that will suggest to students that he may be a member of the school of thought, or participate in the scholarly tradition, defined by that academic or thinker. In addition, if the author thanked another academic for checking over the manuscript before publication, this could possibly indicate an allegiance and shared perspective that may become more apparent when you later become acquainted with that academic's contribution to the debate. Although there are exceptions, you will generally find that, for example, Marxist and other left-wing scholars will primarily liaise with fellow leftists, while scholars working in, for example, a pluralist tradition will predominantly liaise with similarly like-minded academics. With this information you can begin to group the academics and other authors into networks or schools of thought or scholarly traditions such as, for example, being either Marxists or pluralists, or as being defined by the political divisions of Left or Right. Later, in your essay you may want to contrast the findings of Marxist or pluralist scholars or the analyses of left or right-wing commentators.

The preface or introduction to a book will often tell you what the author hoped to achieve, and reading it is an essential part of acquainting yourself with a text. Unfortunately, too many students skip reading this material and therefore miss major clues as to how the book can assist them. Rather than being an optional extra, students should treat this material as essential reading. For example, the vague title of the book by Hugh V. Emy and Owen Hughes, *Australian Politics: Realities in Conflict*, second edition, does not give many clues as to its usefulness. Yet, its brief Preface and Introduction are far clearer. They indicate that the book provides undergraduates with a comprehensive introduction to how the Australian political system works, including a detailed theoretically informed explanation of the ideological and policy framework of the Australian political debate, with special consideration given to the situation in the

1980s and early 1990s when the Hawke Labor Government was in office. This suggests that it could therefore possibly be an opportune place to start a broad study of public policy during the Hawke Government, later turning to the collection edited by Jennett and Stewart to provide details in specific policy areas.

Scanning the chapter headings of a book will also help you to determine its contents. If you find chapters that deal directly with the topic you are investigating, then it may be a useful book, if not, then it may be one to dismiss. If you are still a little unsure of the value of the book, skim read through the chapters until you become more aware of their contents. This is a process that mostly involves scanning the subheadings as well as key words and sentences, while pausing every so often to look more closely at an illustration or graph or to read some passages more carefully as you seek to attain the gist of what is being covered. While engaged in this important process it helps to pay special attention to the introductory chapter and conclusion, because these chapters state the main points of the author's argument or summarise the principal findings. You should also give additional attention to the chapters that deal specifically with the topic in which you are interested.

While we are on the subject of scanning or skim reading, it is helpful to point out that there is no such thing as 'speed reading', which is the study skills equivalent of a get-rich-quick scheme. Speed reading is impossible unless you can speed think. Put another way, you can only read as fast as you can comprehend. The idea that students can run their eyes back and forth for a few seconds along a page of complex philosophy or economic analysis and understand it is fanciful. Nevertheless, it is possible to read faster, an ability that comes with knowledge or experience. Expect to read at a slower pace when the material is new to you or complex. Yet if you already have established substantial layers of knowledge on the topic or if the material is straightforward you will be able to comprehend it faster and consequently read it faster, and over time your reading speed will increase even more as you become more experienced at research.

The process of scanning and skim reading a text is not meant to produce a comprehensive understanding of its contents. Rather, it is the principal way in which you will assess the value of a text so you may, if you later choose to do so, read it more closely to gain a more comprehensive understanding. In addition to this, students may also consider checking the bibliography to determine how extensive or comprehensive it is or what kind of sources were used, with a predominance of primary sources often indicating the originality of the author's research. You may also notice, as you scan a number of the bibliographies among the relevant books and articles that you found, whether some texts are cited more often, which can be a clue as to the importance of these texts in this area of study. If the academics working in this area generally find a text to be indispensable, this may be a clue that it may also be worthwhile for students to consult this text as well. Furthermore, if you also scan the patterns of citation in the footnotes or endnotes you may obtain an even clearer sense of the materials that an author relied upon, which may help you decide what materials you will rely upon. The more experienced students who are already quite familiar with the literature in a particular area will get more out of this process of scanning a bibliography, or footnotes or endnotes, with the most knowledgeable students possibly being able to approximately determine the contents of the book or article from scrutinising which texts are cited as well what is noticeably omitted.

When the process of scanning and skimming leads you to the first text that seems to be perfectly suited to your requirements, the feeling can be exhilarating and liberating. Suddenly you have your initial glimpse of light at the end of the tunnel. As you continue through this stage of the research process, you will eventually be able to divide your pile of potential sources into three sections: those few texts that are essential that will be consulted first, the others that are useful but less important that will be consulted afterwards, and those that are rejected. As a result, the fog of uncertainty lifts to reveal a clearer picture of precisely the materials from which you need to take notes to complete this essay.

The most valuable texts that will receive most of your note-taking attention are usually those that are particularly insightful, ideally providing a great deal of evidence that you can extract and use in your argument. Another very useful type of text includes a review of the literature on the topic thereby providing valuable summaries of the major contributions to the academic debate. This can allow you to gain a breadth of knowledge that comes from having read widely even though you have, understandably, not had time to read all the significant texts. Later, after you have taken notes from these texts, you will take less detailed notes from the sources in the less important group. This group may include books or journal articles that precisely focus on specific aspects of the topic you are researching or texts that mostly repeat material found in your preferred sources except for a few useful additional items. This group may also include a number of the primary source documents, discussed in the secondary sources, which may reveal some additional insights when examined directly. It may also include the original texts that were discussed and summarised in the secondary text that you found that reviewed the significant literature on the topic, sources from which you may derive some additional material or double check the accuracy of the summaries.

After returning the materials that you will not need to their shelves, borrow or photocopy the materials that you do need. When photocopying from a source, do so systematically rather than erratically so you come away with material that you can fully understand. This means that when photocopying an article, you make sure you do not skip photocopying its bibliography, which contains valuable information that adds to one's understanding of the article. Similarly, if you are photocopying a chapter of a book you should not skip pages that you initially assume are not important. Photocopy the whole chapter so it reads as it was intended to read. Moreover, I suggest that you go even further in your thoroughness. If you need to photocopy a chapter from a book, you should also copy the book's title and list of chapters, the introduction, bibliography, the endnotes for that chapter and also maybe even its index, so you can make proper sense of the material in that chapter by obtaining a sense of the context in which that extracted chapter originally appeared and have at your disposal all the other elements of the book that enhance your appreciation of its contents.

Closer reading of the principal sources

Although you have become acquainted with a number of texts relevant to the topic and collected the sources from which you will derive your answer to the assigned essay question, as yet you have probably not come up with your answer, although you may already be forming one. To reach the point where you can form a contention and mount an argument, you need to closely read the texts that you have designated as your principal sources. As you read, you need to have several purposes in mind. Firstly, and most importantly, you should be thinking about the essay question for which you are seeking an answer. Secondly, you need to determine the original purpose of the author for the text that you are reading. If the purpose was different to that for which you are using the book, it is appropriate to acknowledge this in your essay. This information also keeps your research anchored so you do not accidentally mislead yourself as to the meaning of the text that you have used. Thirdly, you also need to bear in mind that you are preparing yourself and the text for the detailed note-taking that will follow this purposeful exploratory reading.

Begin this reading by starting with the text that you perceive to be potentially the most useful. As you read it, use a pencil to underline and annotate, as well as jot down any additional ideas on a handy note pad that rush to your mind that could help you to formulate an answer. Your markings and annotations should take two forms. One form involves underlining or annotating important sentences or passages that either indicate the author's meaning or constitute material that you may find useful. The second form involves writing a word or two near each paragraph, or sequence of related paragraphs, to indicate what they cover to make it easier to navigate through the material later when you take your notes. While we are discussing marking texts, I should point out that it is important to respect books. If you are marking a book that is your property, discreetly use a pencil, which can later be erased to restore it to something close to its original condition. Fluorescent highlighters permanently damage a book and they are best avoided. They also make it difficult to photocopy the highlighted words and they destroy the resale value of the book. Library books should never be marked. So if you feel you need to mark a borrowed text you should instead consider photocopying the sections that you need so you can mark them as you require. Alternatively, you can, if you wish, avoid marking a text altogether by making some brief notes on a pad as to the contents of various pages, which can later serve to guide you through the material.

You should keep reading the texts that you have designated as potentially the most useful until you feel you have become knowledgeable enough to form a contention and mount an argument in support of that contention, although you should appreciate that these early impressions may need to be modified as you progress through subsequent phases of writing the essay. It is difficult to say precisely what is the appropriate amount of purposeful exploratory reading to undertake. You can usually tell when you have done enough when you have an urge to progress to the next stage of writing the essay, since you are becoming keen to express your answer. While being crucial to essay writing, there are some potential pitfalls in this phase of the research process that should be avoided. If the topic is particularly interesting, some students can find this reading so enjoyably fascinating that they seek to prolong it, becoming so immersed that they lose track of their original purpose of producing an essay. If you become aware that this has happened, simply stop and move on to the next phase of the project. Moreover, while purposeful exploratory reading usually leads to a degree of enlightenment to enable students to produce an essay, when taken past a certain point this reading can add confusion by overburdening the mind with too much information from too many sources, consequently delaying the production of the essay. If this happens, it may be opportune to backtrack to the point before when you became confused, then move on from that point to the next phase of producing the essay.

Note-taking for research

After a sufficient amount of purposeful exploratory reading, the next phase of research is note-taking. **The purpose of note-taking from a text is to extract what you need so that it is no longer necessary to keep referring to that text, instead relying on the notes, and a common sense appreciation of this purpose will guide you to take notes effectively.** You would have noticed that I have used the term note-taking rather than summarising, which specifically refers to the abridging or shortening of the material, possibly while converting it into your own words as many teachers encourage their students to do. Note-taking can often involve summarising but on many occasions it may not. Note-taking involves extracting the relevant and useful information that you need to facilitate both an understanding of the text and to provide the raw material from which you will fashion an essay response or produce exam study notes. This material has to be comprehensible and usable. As a result, sometimes this will involve summarising as you seek out the essential elements of what has been stated. But on other occasions it will involve elaboration, making the information longer as you add further explanation to what may have originally been overly concise or complex or poorly expressed material, to make it clearer. Clarity is crucial in note-taking. Sometimes it will be opportune to rephrase the material as you take notes, yet on other occasions this may be counter-productive, so you are better off simply copying out a section of the text in exactly the words in which it originally appeared. This is the most effective and intelligent way to take notes when the original material is subtly nuanced or expressed with such instructive clarity that to tamper with its wording risks producing inexact or inferior notes that could later lead to an inaccurate analysis when you later reflect upon the material or confusion when you draft your essay. Plagiarism is unethical in essays and published work. Yet paranoia about plagiarism is also wrong since it can lead students to create inaccurate notes so the analysis in their essays proceeds from an unsound basis. At the note-taking stage, do not worry about plagiarism. Instead, focus on taking accurate notes that do justice to the meaning of the material. When you eventually write the essay, by reworking the material to suit your specific argument and purposes, it will usually bear little or no resemblance to the original phrasing in the original source. Furthermore, the material that you may decide to quote directly would be scrupulously attributed and footnoted.

Not all of your notes should be confined to reflecting the contents of the source. Because note-taking invites you to become intimately engaged with the contents of a text, you should find yourself stimulated by the material to have ideas of your own about the topic. You may be, for example, inspired to analyse some data in ways that differ from the commentary that accompanied it in the source. Make sure you record these ideas as well, noting the page numbers where the material was found that inspired your own analysis, while at the same time taking care to distinguish your ideas from other notes that deal directly with the contents of the text. These ideas often become central to your argument, and some of them may later stand out as some of the most interesting and important aspects of your essay. So, if you have an inspired rush of ideas, treat this material as just as valuable or more valuable than the material derived from the sources being studied.

Note-taking can easily become confused, especially when it involves numerous or lengthy sources, unless it follows a rigorous procedure. When you begin taking notes from a text, label the top of the first page with the author's name and the title of the text, after that just the author's name at the top of each page will suffice unless you will be taking notes from more than one text by the same author. In addition to labelling, make sure you number all the pages of your notes to enable you to keep track of the order in which you extracted the material. When you extract information, first note the page number and author's surname in the margin of the page on your note pad (for example: Emy and Hughes, p. 111.) then write your notes. Alternatively, you may choose to record this information about the source at the end of the section of notes that you have taken (for example: Emy and Hughes, pp. 111-112). Remember, it is important to mention both the author and page number so this information does not become lost if you later cut and paste or reshuffle the material by putting the notes drawn from one text on an aspect of a topic with notes drawn from another text on the same aspect. If you constantly keep track of this information throughout the note-taking and drafting phases of producing the essay, making accurate footnotes will be a mere formality rather than a source of confusion. There are other reasons why the note-taking process needs to be fastidious.

Your notes should facilitate clear thinking and intelligent reflection about the nature of the topic, so anything that could compromise that process should be avoided. With this principle in mind, it is helpful if you write only on one side of the paper. This produces several significant benefits. Firstly, it means that your pages of notes will not have that muddy appearance that results when the handwriting on one side of the paper is faintly visible when viewed from the other side, so your notes will be more pleasant to read. More importantly, it will allow you to see all the information recorded on that page at a glance, instead of allowing 50 per cent of it to remain concealed on the underside of the paper when you place it on the desk in front of you to reflect upon its contents. Even more importantly, it will allow you to cut and paste material or reshuffle the pages of information when you later need to reorganise the notes so that all the material on the same aspect of the topic drawn from different sources is placed together. Otherwise, any material recorded on the other side of the pages would be damaged or disorientatingly disorganised.

With this principle in mind, it will also help if you clearly and frequently label the content of the extracted information with subheadings, write in full legible sentences as much as possible, avoid making any customised shorthand abbreviations of key words, and space the material on the page so it does not appear confusingly congested. It will also help when you start taking notes from a new chapter, or on a new aspect of the topic, if you start on a new page. In addition, it will help even more if you write in a fashion to avoid allowing a paragraph of your notes to run from one page onto the next. This allows you to keep the idea expressed in that paragraph intact, so it can be seen in total in front of you without having to fuss about by turning a page back and forth, a process that may compromise your ability to concentrate on that idea if you later need to pause and reflect upon its significance. This point is also important when producing notes to study for exams. The information in your exam study notes will be more accessible if it allows you to focus on an idea expressed in a paragraph without having to turn a page, a process that may marginally interfere with the learning process or inhibit your ability to intellectually grapple with complex material.

To effectively take notes from a chapter in a book, you need to read the chapter first and underline and annotate what you perceive to be important passages, if you have not done so already during your purposeful exploratory reading. This initial reading will make your note-taking faster and more effective because it will give you an understanding of the material and an awareness of where the most helpful material is located to enable you to be more astute in your selection from this material. You may discover, for example, that the author virtually summarised his argument at the end of the chapter, which is where the most advantageous note-taking opportunities are found, saving you the trouble of attempting to summarise the earlier more detailed material. Interestingly, you will probably notice that during your second reading of the chapter, you will become aware of additional material that you initially did not realise was important. This is because your first reading added another layer to your knowledge, which in turn facilitated a deeper understanding of the material when you read it again to take notes. Put another way, if students take notes when they first read the chapter, omitting a second reading, they will be more likely to take longer, or become confused, or miss material that is important.

If you follow this procedure you will produce notes from each source that read coherently, are well spaced, have their contents clearly identified with subheadings, and are thoroughly and accurately documented in terms of listing the authors and page numbers associated with each piece of information. As a consequence, the notes from each text should read well individually as documents that outline the meaning of their source and also contain the material that you have found to be useful for the purposes of your project. In addition, the notes for each source should lend themselves to being integrated with your notes from the other sources with each section of the notes maintaining their coherence when placed in a new context. This quality will allow you to reflect intelligently upon this material, as well as later reorganise it into a sequence that can be reworked into an essay. Another beneficial consequence of working with the material in this fashion, is that you would have become much more knowledgeable and better able to analyse and argue effectively with it. You would have also formed a contention and acquired a sense of how your argument will proceed. When you have achieved this, you are ready to write. Even though you may not as yet have taken notes from the less important sources, do not worry, they can efficiently be factored in later once you have a draft.

Note-taking for shorter essays

The research methods that I have taught you are very thorough and precise, and they are ideally suited to effectively handling major essays (ranging from about 2,000-10,000 words) because it will allow you to produce substantial notes from lengthy or numerous sources without becoming confused while working over a considerable time frame (of a week to several months). However for small projects, for example if you have to write a short essay (ranging from about 600-1,500 words) from evidence drawn from a few short newspaper articles, perhaps under exam conditions, there is a much quicker approach. First, read through the articles, underlining and annotating everything that you feel is important or may be of use. This allows you to virtually transform these original documents into something you can use in the same way that you would use notes because you can choose, from that point on, to focus on the underlined and annotated material, ignoring the rest. Nevertheless, if you feel you may need to reread any of these documents to deepen your understanding, then you can do this as well. Take care to record any additional ideas that you have regarding your contention and argument on separate pieces of paper. It is important to write on one side only so you can see at a glance all the relevant information you need to use. When you have organised that underlined and annotated material into a coherent sequence by marking each piece sequentially with letters or numbers (either: a, b, c, d, e, etc., or: 1, 2, 3, 4, 5, etc.), you are ready to write the essay.

Organising study notes for exams

To prepare an effective set of exam study notes on a topic you need to synthesise the notes taken from different sources so they tell one story. If you leave the material as several sets of notes about the same topic, then later study each of them in turn the day before your exam, rather than each set of notes reinforcing the knowledge provided by the previous set, each subsequent set that you look at tends to have the unfortunate effect of negating some of the understanding that you gained from the previous set of notes, leading to confusion and sowing the seeds for disconcerting memory lapses during the exam. To help to prevent this, you need to reorganise and rework the material. Take the material derived from each of your sources about the same aspect of the topic and place them together. Do this for every aspect of the topic that is covered by the notes. Then rewrite the notes, synthesising the sources, so they become one comprehensive set of notes that does not repeat itself, although it may acknowledge that different scholars or commentators had different perspectives or analyses on different aspects of the topic. An additional benefit arising from this rewriting process is that you would have dramatically improved your understanding of the topic and found that you have memorised a great deal of this material without even having tried, which is a pretty advantageous position to be in before an exam.

More advanced modes of research

The research techniques that I have described in this chapter are ideal for effectively dealing with most senior high school and undergraduate essays or for preparing exam study notes. This is because most assignment and exam questions require students to draw on sources derived from the world of organised knowledge (such as books, articles, and published primary documents or survey data) to answer set questions. In addition, the performance of these tasks is usually severely constrained by the limitations of time and word length restrictions. However, some undergraduate projects, as well as research for an Honours, Masters or Doctoral thesis, require students to produce research that adds something new to the world of organised knowledge, and for these projects students are usually afforded the latitude of the additional necessary time and space needed to undertake such a rewarding endeavour.

These students can and should go much further in their pursuit of good scholarship, by adopting more advanced approaches that are akin to those of professional researchers. These students may begin by consulting informative secondary sources to establish an understanding of the topic, the state of the relevant academic debate, and to define their research objectives and appropriate methods. Following this initial round of research, they would, from this sound basis, go further by, for example, gathering various original texts and primary documents (which may include new or unpublished evidence or data) to enable them to deepen their understanding. Unlike the second round of research for most senior high school or undergraduate essays that is intended to complement the initial research from the most useful secondary sources, the second round of research in these more demanding projects needs to be far more extensive. It should, to a significant degree, surpass the initial findings of the original round of research. In a sense, the project really gets under way at this second stage.

For example, when undertaking this second round of research, the researcher would compile the necessary original texts or primary documents and systematically organise them into sections or categories, either chronologically or thematically depending on the researcher's purpose or what allows the researcher to make greater sense of the material. The researcher then closely examines this material, proceeding section by section, taking notes, analysing, problem-solving, interpreting, explaining, synthesising or theorising until each section of the project is resolved. It should be noted that this good scholarship often requires the researcher to critically evaluate and test the evidence, perhaps by checking the validity of the sources or by cross-referencing evidence to determine that each item is validated by other relevant items before it is deemed to be credible. It should also be noted that while this close examination of the material and critical evaluation of the evidence is crucial at the postgraduate level, this process can be a significant contributor to producing high-quality essays at all senior levels in the education system, secondary, undergraduate and postgraduate.

There are sound scholarly reasons why it is better to consult primary source documents rather than rely upon the secondary commentaries and quotations found in secondary sources. There are also sound scholarly reasons why it is better to have consulted the original texts by the original authors that articulated particular theories rather than relied upon a secondary source that summarised and commented upon a number of theories. It is also sound for scholarly reasons why wide reading is beneficial. If one bases one's findings on primary documents or original texts one avoids the risk of being misdirected or misled by the perspectives or mistakes of predecessors, while availing oneself the opportunity to approach the primary subject matter from a new perspective to perhaps reveal new insights. Meanwhile, wide reading allows a scholar to deal comprehensively with a topic to benefit from most, or all, of the relevant material that is available to assist scholars in their deliberations. The process involved in this advanced form of research can be appreciated as like an archaeological excavation, which proceeds in layers, systematically digging deeper and deeper in search of answers. What should emerge from this painstaking but often rewarding process, is an essay that says something new and interesting about its subject, producing well-documented findings that are based largely on primary evidence.

As I stated earlier, these advanced methods of research are more suited to the demands of postgraduate projects. However, for some particularly ambitious undergraduates who are either seeking a High Distinction or to enhance their intellectual creativity and skill, they may seek to incorporate elements of this approach into a project. They may begin by consulting the most helpful secondary sources to establish the basis of their understanding of the topic, then instead of merely enhancing this understanding with additional primary sources, they would substantially deepen their exploration by gathering more primary sources or by examining them more closely with the aim of producing findings that are penetratingly insightful and therefore more scholarly.

Dealing with difficult texts

Before we move on to learn the art of essay writing, it is necessary to discuss a couple of challenging situations that can emerge during research. One of them is how to deal with a text that is extremely difficult to understand. **One of the first things to recognise is that if you have difficulty with a text it may not be your fault. Nevertheless, the responsibility to do something about the situation rests with you.**

If you have difficulty with a text about which you have to write an essay, for example an arcane jargon-laden work of postmodern philosophy that you find to be intellectually impenetrable, there are more effective alternative strategies than repeatedly rereading the text in the agonised hope that you will eventually comprehend it. One way around the problem is to find summaries or commentaries by expert academics on that difficult text and read those. So instead of reading that text you read about that text. If you wish, you may return to the baffling original source, armed with your additional knowledge, and have another attempt at understanding it. This time, you will probably be far more successful.

Why are some texts so difficult to understand? There are several possible reasons. Sometimes it is because they are badly written. Unfortunately, not all academics have writing abilities to match their academic abilities and this can make their arguments difficult to follow. Sometimes texts may be philosophically of a poor quality, so they confuse and obscure more than they enlighten, and this is why students find them difficult. Sometimes a text is difficult to understand because the author deliberately sought to be obscure because he subscribes to what I term the 'cult of the obscure', an affliction that can affect a number of academics and other intellectuals.

But why would some academics, who number among those who are supposedly the community's generators and custodians of knowledge, be content to be or seek to be difficult to understand? Here is a possible explanation. One way to view these academics is as belonging to an elite club of cognoscenti (wise people who believe they have good taste in art, literature and learning), and one way in which they regulate the membership of this club is to challenge potential entrants as to whether they can understand certain material. This language and the texts written in this language are status markers that serve as an effective way of separating the knowing from the unknowing, the included from the excluded. Another possible explanation is that some of these academics, who are acclimatised to being among the cognoscenti, write primarily with their peers in mind as their audience rather than students or the public. They feel so comfortable writing in the jargon of their discipline that they would find it difficult to adopt a more accessible style. Consequently, some students reading this material can find themselves feeling like outsiders looking in at part of a conversation that is difficult to follow and to which they were not invited.

Students who suspect that their examiner is an academic who subscribes to the cult of the obscure may find it advantageous to learn enough of their examiner's preferred form of language to make the appropriate positive impression by using that jargon in their essay. Regardless of whether students find texts written in this form of language challenging, intriguing or annoying, they do not have to allow this kind of material to intimidate them.

If the reason why a text is difficult to understand lies with the student, there is no shame in this either. Instead, there are different approaches to dealing with the situation. As I have stated earlier, people do not become experts straight away and they learn at different rates. If you come across some difficult material, do not let it bother you. Instead, reassure yourself that although it is difficult now it probably will not remain this way as you progress further in your studies and your knowledge and experience increases. Sometimes it may be opportune to try to avoid assignments that involve this difficult material, bypassing it until later in the year or next year when you will be better equipped to try again. If this material is unavoidable and crucial to the course, then you should try everything possible to make it comprehensible, such as by consulting alternative texts that explain the material more clearly, or by seeking the help of knowledgeable classmates or of a private tutor until the problem is overcome. If difficulties persist, then this may be an opportune wake-up call suggesting that you may be in a course that is not in tune with your talents, and a change of direction may be required.

Researching without a reading guide

Apart from difficult texts, the other major challenging situation that students can be confronted with regarding research is to be assigned a topic or question and be expected to produce an essay without the assistance of a reading guide to orient them to sources. This can be a scary prospect for many students, yet the solution is easier than they assume. The simplest way to address this problem is to compensate for it by finding an alternative reading guide. If, for example, you have been assigned a political science question on a topic in American politics and the university politics course did not furnish you with a reading guide to assist your entry into the literature, you may overcome this by walking over to the American history department and purchasing their reading guide to take advantage of a section in it that is relevant to your topic. Similarly, you could go to another university with a similar course and purchase their reading guide, and use that to help you get started. Moreover, with the advent of the internet, you can avoid the footwork, since many universities post their course outlines and reading guides on the web where they can be of assistance to anyone who is seeking a systematic appreciation of the literature on the topics covered in these guides. There are other approaches to this problem.

Alternatively, you may scour library databases for a text that reviews the literature in this field and then use that review as your guide into this literature. In addition, if there are relevant Masters or Doctoral theses at your university, which are stored separately to the main collections in the library, they can be useful in this regard because it is compulsory for postgraduate students to include a literature review in their thesis. So, why not capitalise on their path finding efforts? On the other hand, you could locate a text on your topic (such as an introductory textbook) and use its bibliography as a reading guide to help you determine the significant literature in this field.

Getting started on an unguided research project is more difficult than other projects and it takes more time. It involves more purposeful exploratory reading than is required for guided projects, to orient you towards the nature of your topic and the way the literature is organised before you can begin the specific research directed towards answering your question. However, once you have achieved this necessary degree of orientation, your work can proceed in the same fashion as it would with any other essay. **When autonomously exploring a subject that is new to you, it will help you to adhere to the following simple rules with your reading: start general and progress to the particular, begin basic and progress to the advanced.** Use general or introductory textbooks as a guide and source of orientation towards the subject, which is their principal purpose. They will include material that can guide you towards the most significant texts in this area. Then from there, you can progress to the more specialised texts, which in turn will provide the basis for you to progress in your reading to the more advanced texts.

These simple rules are profoundly liberating. With them, you can become autodidactic, which means you have the ability to educate yourself after you complete your formal studies, an ability from which you can prosper all you life. This quality is the ultimate goal because it means that you can make the vast world of knowledge your friend, and what a formidable friend it will be. You will be empowered, free from having to rely on any education institution in your pursuit of knowledge. Formal education has a great many benefits to offer, apart from bestowing qualifications, but when you have the capacity to be autodidactic, you can utilise its institutions as a matter of choice rather than need. **If you can educate yourself, you are firmly in the driver's seat of your life and in control of your destiny.**

We have already learnt many of the valuable skills that contribute to students making the transition to being in control of their destinies, yet there are several more to cover. Having learnt the art of research, it is appropriate that we turn to the art of essay writing.

Becoming accomplished: The art of essay writing

Understanding the structure of essays

The first step to mastering this crucial form of expression, which will be used to obtain many or most of your grades in many subjects at school or university, is to appreciate why the essay has its particular structure, which consists of the following four parts:
- the introduction,
- the body,
- the conclusion, and
- the bibliography (which is optional for some essays).

You would have probably been told by many teachers that essays must conform to this structure, but you have probably never been told why and therefore never fully understood why you needed to adhere to it. This probably meant that the nature of the essay remained mysterious. I intend to unravel that mystery for you because this degree of understanding is not simply important to help you to write essays but essential to help you to write them well, which is our objective.

The major clue as to why essays have their particular structure is found in a term that you would have heard many times before in class – 'argumentative essay'. Put simply, an essay is an argument. By that I am not referring to the more common use of the term as meaning a dispute between two or more parties, but rather to the philosophical meaning of the term, which is when a contention is supported by reason and evidence. You have probably noticed that some teachers may have also referred to 'explanatory', 'analytical' or 'expository' essays, etc., as if these were completely different varieties. Unfortunately, if these distinctions are taken too far, they can be misleading. If you think about them carefully, you will notice that each of these varieties usually expects you to mount a logical argument, just as a so-called argumentative essay does. Taking the example of the explanatory essay, the explanation is the argument or rather the argument that is mounted is that which offers the best explanation. Similarly, an analysis or exposition usually presents an answer that is supported by reasons. In other words, it is presented as an argument. Even though there are instances where explanations, analyses and expositions are expressed in ways that merely state the obvious rather than present arguments, it will nevertheless greatly help you in your quest for mastery in essay writing to think of each of these varieties as merely variations on a theme, this original theme having been defined by the argumentative essay. You will have a clearer understanding and a greater control over your essay writing if you treat all essays as if they are argumentative essays, even 'creative' essays, which can be seen as arguments expressed in a more abstract form. Although some creative writing can be unorthodox or experimental, it can generally be appreciated that for creative writing to be valued as literature it must have something to say about the nature of the world or the human condition. Yet, instead of making most of its points directly, as would be the case in an argumentative essay, the writer creates characters, situations and settings that imply these points indirectly. The readers' interpretation of the meaning of these characters, situations and settings is meant to produce the argument in abstract, so if the meaning of the creative writing is readily comprehensible, the writer's argument is understood. Now that we appreciate that, in general, essays present arguments and that it is advantageous for us to appreciate essays in this fashion, let us look more closely at the nature of an argument.

If we look closely at how an argument is expressed formally in philosophy, it will provide us with some profound clues as to why the essay has its particular structure. Here is a classic example of a deductive argument:

>   Premise 1:   All men are mortal.
>   Premise 2:   Socrates is a man.
>   Conclusion: Therefore Socrates is mortal.

You will notice in the above example that each premise in the argument makes a point, and each point flows logically to the conclusion. You would also notice that the conclusion sums up the argument without introducing any new evidence. Does this sound familiar? At this point, you may recall that many teachers have probably told you that the conclusion to an essay sums up the argument without introducing any new evidence. That is correct, but now you know why. It is because an essay can be seen as an elaborate version of the kind of argument illustrated above. At this stage it is opportune to acknowledge that in addition to the form of deductive argument that I have used in the above example, there are also several forms of inductive arguments, and to avoid complicating matters we shall look at those later. It will serve us better for now to use this deductive argument as our model through which we can understand the structure of essays.

Let us look even closer at the structure of this argument and its instructive similarities to the structure of the essay. It will help, for now, for us to think of the introduction as something added to the front of the essay, like an overture to an opera or ballet, which establishes the main melodic themes but without the actual opera or ballet commencing. Similarly, let us for now think of the bibliography as something added to the end of the essay, like the credits that run at the end of a film. Although we shall later examine in detail these important components, for now we shall put them aside and focus on the body and conclusion, because it is the relationship between these parts that provides the most revealing clues as to why the essay has its particular structure.

You would have noticed that each paragraph in an essay makes a point, which, of course, is the purpose of a paragraph. These points flow logically in succession: for example, paragraphs one, two, three, four, five, six, seven and eight leading to the concluding paragraph. You would have also noticed that each premise in a formal argument makes a point, and each point flows logically in succession to the conclusion. Now can you see the similarity in the structure? Each paragraph can be seen as a point just like a point in a formal argument, and these points (or paragraphs) flow logically to the conclusion. The essay derives its structure from the formal argument in philosophy or, put another way, the essay is simply a more elaborate form of this argument. Hopefully, after having learnt this, writing an essay should already seem easier to you. If when presented with a question, you think of, for example, eight points that support your answer, you simply arrange them in an appropriate order and they become the paragraphs of your essay. You may have already been doing this instinctively, but now that you understand the logical formula, you will soon be able to write with far greater control and virtuosity.

There is more that we can learn from the structure of a formal argument. You may have noticed that it also determines the structure of books, for example: chapters one, two, three, four, five, six, seven and eight flowing logically to the concluding chapter. We can even see the same structure repeated again in multi-volume texts, for example: volumes one, two, three, four, five, six, seven and eight flowing logically to the concluding volume. The example of a formal argument that I presented to you earlier can serve as a formula to unlock for you the mystery as to why essays, books, and multi-volume texts share a particular structure. Despite these revelations, this example of a formal argument can do even more for us. It can help to explain the structure of individual paragraphs.

A paragraph usually consists of several sentences that each make minor points that contribute to making a main point. This main point can be made at the beginning, somewhere in the middle, or at the end of the paragraph. If we look again at the example of the formal deductive argument, we can observe that it structurally resembles a three sentence paragraph that makes its main point in its closing sentence:

> Premise 1: All men are mortal.
> Premise 2: Socrates is a man.
> Conclusion: Therefore Socrates is mortal.

Traditionally, essays strictly observe this structure in this order, although within paragraphs it is permissible to rearrange the order of the premises and the conclusion. Logically this is possible because the soundness of the argument does not require these components to be always expressed as a sequence of premises leading to the conclusion. Instead, you may place the conclusion first, or in the middle of the premises, as well as at the end of the sequence. Similarly, within the paragraph, for example, you can have the main point of the paragraph followed by a supporting sentence and then another supporting sentence. Alternatively, you could have a supporting sentence, then state the main point, then have another supporting sentence. The versatility of the logical structure of the argument can be illustrated by the fact that you can even reduce the premises and conclusion to a diagram:

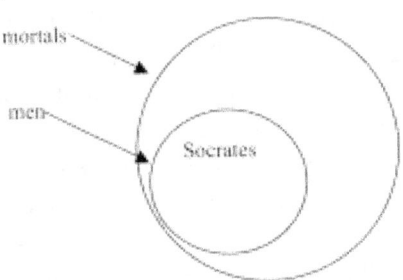

We can see in the diagram that, according to the first premise, everything in the set of men is also in the set of mortals. We can see that, according to the second premise, Socrates is in the set of men. Consequently, we can also see the conclusion illustrated in the diagram. If everything in the set of men is in the set of mortals, and Socrates is *in the set of men, then he* must also be in the set of mortals. Therefore, he must be mortal. The diagram helps to illustrate the fact that each of the premises and the conclusion make sense regardless of the order in which you read them.

Generally speaking, each paragraph of an essay can be seen as a mini-argument that comes to a conclusion and therefore makes a point. This conclusion or point then becomes a premise in the overall argument of the essay, with the points made by each paragraph successively leading to the conclusion of the essay.

The introduction of an essay

Now that we understand the logic that explains the structure of an essay that is evident in the body and conclusion, we can turn to examining another important part of the essay, the introduction. This is a specialist component, used to commence the essay, which has to achieve several tasks intended to enhance the readers' appreciation of the argument. Firstly and most importantly, it has to state the author's contention. I have already used the term 'contention' several times in this discussion of the nature of the essay, yet it is a term that is not commonly used so it may help you to become more comfortable with it if I remind you of some more commonly used synonyms. Another word for contention is answer. The statement of your contention can simply be the statement of your answer to the question, which may be as straightforward as the word 'yes'. Other synonyms for the word contention are: belief, opinion, claim, main point, viewpoint, position, proposition, or thesis. Some of you may be thinking that the contention is bound to bear a striking resemblance to another part of the essay that we have discussed earlier, that's right – the conclusion. The statement of the contention can be seen as a preview to the conclusion. Alternatively, the conclusion can be seen as a restatement of the contention but with more confidence in the light of the preceding evidence. Now that you are aware of this logical symmetry, writing the conclusions to your essays will be easy. When you reach the end of writing the body of the essay, you merely go back to your introduction and paraphrase the statement of your contention, and it will fit perfectly as your conclusion because logically this has to be the case.

The introduction should also define the key terms that are found in the question and used in the essay. This is important because there can often be a range of definitions or understandings for many terms, so it is essential for students to clarify the way they have understood and used certain terms because this can affect the way their argument is perceived and appreciated. The purpose is to remove any potential ambiguity in the interpretation of the key terms by the audience so they are encouraged to follow the logical flow of the argument as the author intended. There are two types of definitions that students may use. The first type is dictionary-style definitions of the kind that are found in reputable scholarly references and texts. These sources may include the English dictionary, various specialist subject dictionaries or the definitions found in learned books or articles about the topic covered by the essay. However, in a number of circumstances with this type of definition, such as in less formally academic essays, instead of deriving and attributing a definition to a scholarly source it can be sufficient to simply provide a definition of a term that appears as if it could have been derived from a scholarly source. In these circumstances, these definitions are simply stated confidently and clearly, rather than fastidiously attributed or footnoted. The second type of definition is contingent definitions, or what I term tactical definitions. These definitions are for terms that require clarification but not to the extent required by other terms. For example, if students were asked to write an essay about the 'main characters' of a play, it would be unnecessarily pedantic to use the English dictionary to define the words 'main' or 'characters'. However, this term 'main characters' does require clarification. Because it is up to the student to clarify the term in a credible fashion, this affords him some leeway, giving him the opportunity to choose a definition that best suits his purposes. If, for example, the student believes that his case will be best served by maximising the amount of evidence in the play from which he can formulate an argument, he may chose a definition for 'main characters' that includes a substantial number of them. On the other hand, if the student believes that his case is best served by a narrower focus, he may decide to define the term in a fashion that refers to only a few characters.

It should also be noted that students might include among the definitions that they provide in the introduction to their essay an introduction to the topic, which defines or clarifies it. For example, in response to a question about the character Othello the student may begin by pointing out that Othello is the principal character in the tragedy *Othello* by William Shakespeare. In addition, these introductory definitions may include a clarification of the issue at hand that crystallises the requirements of the question. In addition to this, these definitions may include further clarifications of your approach to the question by declaring the parameters of your answer, just as the tactical definition of 'main characters' does by clarifying how many characters will be discussed.

While the statement of the contention and the definition of key terms are regarded as virtually compulsory requirements for an introduction to an essay, another valuable component is a concise outline of the argument to follow. When used, this is the last component expressed in an introduction. It can take a form something like the following: 'This essay shall first examine this, before exploring this, and then finally it will discuss this'. This outline is not necessary for very short essays (of about 600 words), yet it is extremely useful for essays of average or longer lengths because it clearly informs the examiners that you are systematically working your way through the material rather than wandering through the topic. If stated at the end of an introduction, especially a lengthy one, this component also serves to let the examiners know that the introduction has finished and what follows is the body of the essay. Despite these substantial benefits, while tutoring students I have noticed that about a quarter of teachers do not appreciate this component of an introduction, so if you become aware that you have one of these teachers, simply leave it out. Nevertheless, since most teachers do appreciate this outline, it is more advantageous to include it whenever you can, especially in exam responses, where the additional clarification that it provides can add to the positive impression that you want to convey to your examiners that you have a solid command over the topic and a clear structure to your argument.

While the inclusion of a statement of the contention, the definition of key terms, and an outline of what is to follow are usually sufficient for the introductions of most high school and many university essays, there are additional components that may be included in the introductions of a number of university essays. An introduction to these essays may also include a statement of the methodology used to undertake the research, such as describing the question and answer survey used in a social scientific project, or explaining the historical method employed that involved the study of the personal papers and diaries of relevant historical figures, or justifying the form of economic modelling chosen to examine the potential outcomes of a range of policy options. The introduction to certain university essays may also include a statement of the theoretical framework or tradition of inquiry that encompasses the student's approach to the project. This would encourage the examiners to assess students working in, for example, a pluralist tradition, according to the standards and expectations of that tradition rather than by those of another tradition, like Marxism. Finally, the introductions in some university essays may include a review of the significant literature in this field of inquiry, thereby assessing the state of the debate on the topic, noting in particular any gaps or problem areas that justify the contribution made by the student's research. More than any of the other components, this can add considerably to the length of an introduction in a major essay such as an Honours, Masters or Doctoral thesis, sometimes becoming virtually a mini-essay within the essay.

The bibliography of an essay

Now that you understand the components that can be included in the introduction to an essay, it is necessary to examine the bibliography, which is added to the end of the essay. A bibliography alphabetically lists the sources that were consulted or used during the research for non-fiction works. It is different to a reference list that only mentions the works that were cited. Rather than treating this as merely a technical requirement, students should appreciate that the bibliography adds further messages to the end of the argument about the student's credibility to make claims about the topic, and about the nature and quality of the research that can affect the way that the essay's argument is appreciated. With this in mind, students can choose to present a bibliography that focuses precisely on the essential elements or key sources of the topic or one that indicates breadth in its coverage. Focused bibliographies suggest competence in the selection and control of the relevant subject matter, while bibliographies that are more extensive suggest thoroughness, that no stone was left unturned in the quest for answers. Students should be aware that examiners, especially those who are knowledgeable about the subject, often check the student's bibliography first, to gain an initial impression of the nature and quality of the research behind the argument, so it is in the students' best interest to create a positive impression to complement the essay. However, if the examiner does read the bibliography last, or merely glances at it, it is still important that it makes the appropriate positive impression because it is the last thing that they will see before they decide upon your grade.

Citations or footnotes

Similar impressions are created by the use of citations or footnotes. Most students appreciate that they are required to acknowledge the source of a quotation, yet many students do not appreciate how citations can be used more expressively to bolster their arguments. The citation of primary sources can be used to imply that your comments have a formidable foundation and therefore should not be treated lightly, just in case the examiner entertained any doubts. Meanwhile, the citation of secondary sources can be used to suggest to your examiner that your case has considerable backing and others can be seen as standing behind you in making a particular point. Citations should be used to acknowledge, along with quotations, the source of any evidence used in the essay as well as the material from which ideas were derived or that inspired your reasoning. In addition, footnotes can be used for another purpose than citation, to add interesting, relevant but inessential details that if included in the text would have interrupted the flow of the argument; this flow of ideas, of course, being crucial both stylistically and logically to the potential persuasiveness of the argument.

Making a logical argument

Now that we understand the structure of essays, writing them can be reduced to a simple formula that you can use to great success throughout school, university and beyond, but before we learn this formula we should briefly return to learning some more about logic, which provides the foundation of the kind of clear thinking, relevant to all subjects, that you should be expressing in your essays. This information is some of the most valuable that I can share with you to improve the merit of your work in any subject. If you have been taught this indispensable knowledge already, this material will serve as revision in an area that cannot be revised too much. If you have not encountered this before, then this explanation will compensate for that omission. With this knowledge, rather than reason intuitively, you will be able to reason with more control as well as appreciate the arguments of others more perceptively.

Deductive arguments, when they are sound, are appreciated as a persuasive form of reasoning because if the premises are true, and the conclusion follows directly from the premises, then the reasoning is regarded as valid and the conclusion is regarded as inescapably compelling and appreciated as true. This is the case in the example discussed earlier:

> Premise 1: All men are mortal.
> Premise 2: Socrates is a man.
> Conclusion: Therefore Socrates is mortal.

However, a deductive argument can be challenged if it can be shown to be faulty in the way its premises flow to the conclusion or if it has one or more false premises, neither of which is the case in the above example.

Nevertheless, if it is not possible to mount a sound deductive argument, all is not lost. There are other forms of reasoning known as inductive arguments that can be used. With these arguments there is an important difference. If they are expressed in a manner that is cogent (with the conclusion following logically from the premises and the premises being true), their conclusions are perceived as probable rather than inescapable. It should be recognised that strong inductive arguments can present conclusions that are extremely probable. However, it should also be recognised that the conclusions of inductive arguments can vary considerably according to the degree of their probability and therefore the strength of their reasoning. Consequently, their conclusions are usually qualified by terms like 'possibly' or 'probably' or 'most likely' or 'highly likely', etc. There are several forms of inductive arguments and it will be helpful if you become familiar with them.

One widely used form of inductive reasoning is an argument to the best explanation. The premises of these arguments describe facts or regularities that require explanation, and the conclusion provides the explanation, or rather the best possible explanation that is reasonable to derive from the facts. For example:

> Premise 1: While walking home this evening, I saw hundreds of young people, most of whom were wearing black T-shirts, cueing in front of the Palais Theatre.
> Conclusion: There is probably a heavy metal rock concert at the Palais Theatre tonight.

Another form of inductive argument is an inductive generalisation. These are arguments that generalise from information about a sample of some class of entity to reach a conclusion about the whole class of this entity, or for some additional examples that are not included in that sample. For example:

> Premise 1: An opinion poll of a randomly selected representative sample of voters taken just prior to the presidential election revealed that a narrow majority intend to vote for the Republican candidate.
> Conclusion: The Republican candidate will probably win the presidential election.

Another form of inductive reasoning that is closely related to the inductive generalisation is an analogical inference. These arguments start with information about the similarities or shared features of two things or situations and conclude that they share additional similarities or that some additional feature is common to both. Put another way, it is understood that because two things or situations are alike in some respects they may be alike in others. For example:

> Premise 1: Water circulates in pipes due to a pump.
> Premise 2: Blood circulates in veins and arteries in a similar fashion to water in pipes.
> Conclusion: The blood probably circulates in the veins and arteries due to a pump (the heart).

An analogical inference like the one above can imply or infer the likelihood of something, sometimes quite strongly, but it cannot prove something. Further evidence and argument would be required. In addition, the examples used to illustrate an argument to the best explanation and an inductive generalisation can be seen to rely on the appreciation of additional material or concepts that were not stated but understood that make these inductive arguments plausible, such as the nature of youth culture and of the venue in front of which the young people were gathered; or the nature of democratic political procedure and the credibility of scientifically conducted opinion polls. If you wish, when interpreting these arguments you can make them more comprehensible by appreciating this additional information as part of the argument, as unstated premises that are implied by the nature of the subject or the logic of the argument. Furthermore, it should be recognised that while these inductive arguments can be seen as potentially strengthened by the appreciation of relevant material that exists outside the argument, they can also be seen as potentially vulnerable to the introduction of new evidence that may change the way in which they can be rationally appreciated. In the political example above, this could include a more detailed understanding of how the distribution of the votes of US citizens between various states translates into the Electoral College votes that determine the outcome of presidential elections, facts that could introduce more uncertainty regarding the expected outcome.

This discussion of deductive and inductive reasoning should equip you to mount the kind of logical arguments that will provide a sound basis for your essays. With this in mind, we can now turn to learning a simple, easy to follow formula for essay writing that you can employ profitably from now into the future.

The formula for masterful essay writing

Not only is this formula simple and easy to follow, it is liberating. This is because it will remove much of the stress that comes from being uncertain about what to do. Moreover, adhering to the formula will allow you to focus on your creativity and develop your expressive skills to a high standard. The formula is also versatile, providing a framework through which you can effectively communicate the products of your imagination and demonstrate your ability to reason, while still complying with the formal conventions of the essay format.

The formula for masterful essay writing consists of the following phases:

- **First, you address the question that you have been given by underlining and then clarifying the key terms that you may have to define and/or address in your answer.** This ensures that your response to the question is focused precisely on what is required and proceeds from this solid basis.

- **Next, you brainstorm and/or research to gather the information that you need to formulate and support an answer.** When you have developed a contention that can be supported by reason and evidence, you are approaching the 'take off' point, which means you can stop gathering information and start writing.

- **Next, you organise the relevant material into a coherent sequence or outline that will serve as your plan for writing the essay.** Now you are ready to write.

- **Next, you write your introduction.** At this stage, since you have developed and expressed a contention, gathered the relevant supporting information, and organised it into a logical sequence, most of the difficult thinking has been done.

- **Next, you execute the essay following your plan.** Having effectively completed the preceding steps, this will be a relatively straightforward process.

- **Finally, you edit to improve your expression or correct any mistakes as required.**

You can beneficially follow this simple procedure for both assigned essays and exam responses, although for exam responses the process is condensed into a limited time frame. With this formula at your disposal, you are a giant step closer to mastering the art of essay writing, but there is more to learn to consolidate your command over this important expressive medium. We shall now turn to what else is needed to furnish you with this formidable ability by examining in detail several phases of the process of essay writing to show you exactly what is required to excel.

Becoming more accomplished: Additional insights into the art of essay writing

Having covered the basic elements of essay writing and derived a formula, it is opportune to look into the phases of the writing process in more detail to ensure that every aspect of this process can be marshalled to work in your favour.

Scrutinising the question

The first phase of writing an essay, the process of addressing the question, has already been discussed in an earlier section covering research. Nevertheless, there are a few additional valuable points that can be made. The process of underlining the key terms in the question is useful because it helps you to scrutinise the question to determine exactly what is required to answer it. Your answer needs to be focused precisely on the demands of the question because to stray, even marginally, can cost a student heavily in grades, which means that most of a student's painstaking research efforts would have resulted in far less than was hoped for or deserved according to the quality of the material. Students need to avoid the temptation to say all that they know about the topic in their answer. Rarely do questions allow students this opportunity. Instead, be specific and remain focused throughout the essay. While helping students as a private tutor, I have noticed how often even a minor lapse of focus on the requirements of the question can cost students heavily in grades. Although good scholarship requires focusing on the question, it often seemed that the severity of the punishment for these lapses did not fit the crime. You may also have noticed this in your experiences. It can sometimes seem as if some examiners derive some personal satisfaction in catching hapless students who stray marginally from the requirements of the question, as if each discovery provides a boost to their sense of competence as examiners. Interestingly, the examiners who do this may not even be aware of this tendency in themselves. Nevertheless, it is probably the case that in a number of instances, a large deduction of grades may represent a measure of the examiner's own satisfaction in their ability – the more they deduct, the more satisfied that they feel – more than it reflects a precise and proportioned response to the student's error. Consequently, what results too often is a disproportionately severe response to the student's lapse. This is all the more reason to clearly determine the requirements of the question and to remain focused on them.

What is worse, is when an examiner perceives that a student has strayed from the question when this was not the case. To prevent this unfortunate, unfair and costly circumstance, students need to use several terms and phrases derived from the question in the statement of their contention and throughout their essay. This is to clearly signpost the fact to their examiner that they have closely focused on the requirements of the question. Do not be subtle, because subtlety can be overlooked, especially if the examiner is skim reading or disoriented by poor quality handwriting. Instead, light it in neon. **By repeatedly using terms derived from the question throughout your essay, you are not leaving any opportunity for a misinterpretation of your degree of focus on the question.**

Brainstorming

The second phase of writing an essay, the brainstorming and research, has been substantially discussed in the section dealing with the art of research, apart from the important process of brainstorming, to which we will now turn. Brainstorming is researching your own knowledge. Just as research involves gathering information from sources and recording it in notes, so that you no longer need to use those sources and can proceed to write the essay by using your notes, brainstorming involves recording what you know about a topic as notes, then working from those notes. Brainstorming is important for all essays because it is a means of recording your first and any subsequent rush of relevant ideas, which often prove to be quite valuable. It is especially crucial for exam responses, when research is not possible and you need to quickly organise the relevant material that you have learnt so you can respond effectively to the question.

Brainstorming can also be employed to avoid the perils of what I term 'stream of consciousness writing'. This occurs when a student begins writing an essay by stating the first thing that comes to mind, which in turn triggers something else, and something else, and something else, until the student cannot think of anything else to say and concludes the essay. This process often produces poorly structured writing that gives the impression to the examiner that the student is wandering through the topic rather than mounting a coherent argument. This negative impression can be made worse when the most important point that the student thought of, which should have been stated at the beginning of the essay, is the last thing they remembered and mentioned. The examiner of an essay such as this would begin reading, expecting that the most important point would be mentioned early. Then, when they do not find it covered in the introduction or opening paragraphs, they form a negative impression of the essay. Then, as they read further and they still do not find it mentioned, their attitude becomes increasingly critical. When they eventually do come across this point at the end of the essay, this may not redeem the student, because the examiner may become even more annoyed at this late reminder that this crucial point was not mentioned earlier, where it should have been.

This stream of consciousness should be channelled into brainstorming, where it is beneficial, and kept from the writing phase, where it is hazardous. When brainstorming, it does not matter whether your best idea comes to you first or last. Once you have brainstormed, you can organise the material into a coherent sequence and systematically address the topic. As a result, your essay will convey to your examiner that you know exactly what you are doing from the outset, and this positive impression will be reinforced as the essay proceeds in a logical, orderly fashion.

Structure, planning and execution

This discussion of the perils of stream of consciousness writing would have reminded you of the crucial importance of having a clear coherent structure to your essay. This is largely achieved in the planning phase, when you organise the relevant material into a coherent sequence. Our previous examination of the logic that underlies mounting sound arguments would have brought home to you the fundamental importance of this characteristic of persuasive writing. Before you begin drafting, you need to examine the material that you have gathered to devise an effective structure for your essay so your points reach your examiner in the most coherent and persuasive sequence. Only when you have determined this sequence are you ready to start writing. Devising this sequence usually involves commonsense. For example, it makes sense to outline a theory before you discuss its application. Most accounts of events are best explained chronologically. The points in an argument are usually more effective when expressed from the most important to the least important, except when the secondary points logically build up to the most important point.

Furthermore, an additional benefit of having a clear coherent structure is that it will significantly contribute to allowing the quality of your ideas to shine through and be appreciated. If an essay is poorly structured, the examiner can become confused and disoriented, which can lead to the examiner overlooking the value of much of a student's evidence and reasoning. This can result in the awarding of a lower grade than the student deserved according to the quality of the content of the essay. Fortunately, this problem is usually easily rectified by restructuring the essay.

While helping students as a private tutor, I have observed that some examiners are very aware of the importance of essay structure, and they specify this concern when they critically comment on poorly structured work when they make their assessment. However, there are other examiners who also criticise essays with this problem, yet, curiously, they fail to mention the structural flaws among their criticisms. These examiners are interesting because of what their omission reveals about the way that essay structure is psychologically appreciated. When the students of these examiners restructure their formerly poorly structured work and resubmit it as well-structured essays, something interesting can often be observed in these examiners' reactions. The grades go up but, curiously, these examiners often do not praise the second version of the essay for its structure. Instead, they usually praise the content of the second version – content that remained unchanged from the poorly structured version that was initially submitted. It is as if these examiners never noticed this content earlier. This suggests that for a number of examiners, especially those who may assess their students' work quickly, a coherent structure may not be directly appreciated at a conscious level. Instead, a coherent structure makes the essay easier to read and facilitates an appreciation of the quality of the content that would have otherwise been overlooked, allowing the students to be rewarded for this material, as they deserved to be. We can learn much from observing these examiners' behavior. We can learn that the structure or sequence in which ideas are presented affects the way they are perceived. Now that you are aware of this tendency, you can turn it to your advantage by making sure that you coherently structure your work to maximise the appreciation of its content.

You have probably heard many teachers impress on their classes the importance of an essay plan. You now probably realise that they are right, although the reasons that I have provided are probably different to the reasons they provided. I will go one step further, to suggest that in combination with the introduction, the plan can be regarded as more important than the body of the essay itself. Although this is a deliberate exaggeration, it is an instructive one. Once you have effectively planned the essay and written the introduction, the rest can seem like a formality. This is because at that moment when you have determined the points in your argument and outlined the sequence in which you will present them, and once you have carefully composed and expressed your introduction to have stated your contention, defined the key terms used in the essay and outlined the argument that will follow, you have essentially solved the question. This is especially the case with shorter essays such as exam responses. In an exam, once you have brainstormed, planned, and written the introduction, the difficult part is over with, it is just a matter of putting your head down and finishing the essay, executing your plan with confident dexterity.

Writing the body of the essay essentially involves transforming the notes from your research and/or brainstorming that had been organised into different segments, into coherent sections of the essay. Once you have completed a draft that is based on your notes derived from the major sources, you can then enrich its content by factoring in additional material derived from minor sources, which will make your work more thorough and detailed. Furthermore, as you rework the material in your notes from various sources into a coherent argument that supports your contention and precisely answers the essay question, your reworking of this material effectively transforms it into your own words. It may have begun as notes of your ideas accompanied by a series of more extensive notes extracted from sources, but through the writing process, this material has become integrated and transformed into your own argument, which is, of course, based on or supported by relevant sources. You should also be aware that the process of writing can aid the process of analysis, throwing up additional or more perceptive understandings. These insights should be welcomed and incorporated into your essay. You may choose to rewrite, add to, or rearrange sections of the essay, redrafting to enrich the essay's content, improve its coherence or enhance its expressiveness.

Organising the footnotes and bibliography

When you are reasonably satisfied with the draft, you can shift your attention to completing the organisation of your footnotes and bibliography. We have already discussed the footnotes and bibliography in terms of their potential to add further expressive elements to your essay. Now we shall look at them again in terms of their technical requirements. Having taken your notes in a fashion that constantly recorded and kept track of the sources of the information, and having taken care to have continually incorporated this information into the draft, the process of organising your footnotes and bibliography should have already been largely completed except for the fine-tuning to ensure that they conform closely to academic standards.

The technical requirements for making footnotes and bibliographies can be found in style manuals that can be purchased at many academic and university bookstores, while some schools and university departments will supply this information in handouts. You can also find additional guidance by looking at scholarly publications and copying the way they made their references. Several systems are available, so select one that is appropriate to your subject and use it consistently. One of the most popular is the documentary-note system that is used in most humanities and many other subjects. When a student wants to make a citation, either after a key term or at the end of the relevant sentence or paragraph, a footnote number is entered that is situated just above the text, then a corresponding footnote is made at the bottom of the page. It can also appear as an endnote at the end of a chapter or book. The footnote begins with the author's initials and surname, then mentions the title of the text, the publisher, the place of publication, the year of publication, and the relevant page numbers. Each of these pieces of information is separated by commas as if they are phrases in a sentence and the note ends with a full stop. For example:

W. Doyle, *Origins of the French Revolution,* Oxford University Press, Oxford, 1980, p. 40.

The second time that a reference is made to the same text, an abbreviated version of the note is used, for example:

Doyle, pp. 212-213.

Because a bibliography is organised alphabetically, the author's initials are mentioned after the surname, which differs from the footnotes because they are organised numerically. For example:

Doyle, W., *Origins of the French Revolution*, Oxford University Press, Oxford, 1980.

Another popular method is the author-date system that is used in the natural and social sciences and is also quite popular in various humanities subjects. To cite a text, enter, enclosed in brackets, the author's name, the year of publication and the page numbers. For example:

(Corey, 1996, pp. 317-320)

The bibliography is organised alphabetically, as with the documentary-note system, except the date of publication is mentioned just after the author's surname rather than at the end of the reference, to make it easier to identify the relevant bracketed citations in the text of the essay with the corresponding references in the bibliography. For example:

Corey, G., 1996, *Theory and Practice of Counseling and Psychotherapy*, fifth edition, Brooks/Cole, Pacific Grove, California.

Bibliographies and their accompanying footnotes or endnotes are scholarly conventions practised within the academic community to allow scholars to check the research of others or build upon it. Students are expected to show competence in this to demonstrate their potential to operate in the appropriate manner within this community. So it is in the students' interests to purchase a style manual and carefully follow the appropriate rules to convey the appropriate impression of professional aptitude to the examiners. This will help to encourage them to treat your work seriously, rather than as just another student essay.

In addition to the technical requirements of bibliographies, we have also previously discussed how they can be used as an expressive element of your essay to lend additional support to an appreciation of the quality and nature of your research, by being either focused or extensive. Having said this, it should be acknowledged that most examiners are impressed by lengthy bibliographies. Many students quickly become aware of this widespread tendency and, regrettably, some are even tempted to pad their bibliographies. Unfortunately, those students are probably not aware that the obligations of good scholarship require them to provide a full and informative bibliography, a process that has the effect of maximising its length in ways that are both legitimate and academically commendable.

The bibliography should firstly include those few sources that were relied upon to produce most of the research notes and the initial draft. To them would be added the other more numerous but less significant texts that were used to enrich the material derived from the principal sources. Remember, when dealing with anthologies it is both good scholarship and advantageous towards maximising your bibliography to individually list each chapter written by a different author that you used or consulted. You may also choose to treat published collections of documents in the same fashion, except if you consulted so many documents from the same collection that to list each one individually would seem pedantic. Finally, you would add several helpful sources that you consulted while doing your research that contributed to your understanding of the topic but, as it turned out, did not feature in the content of your essay. This process should produce a bibliography that covers, then goes beyond the sources listed in the prescribed reading guide, which is precisely what many examiners like to see and reward.

Meanwhile, the footnotes to the initial draft of your essay will firstly appear repetitive, referring often to those few most helpful texts that enabled you to produce this draft. However, as you enrich your essay by adding to it your findings from various minor sources, this pattern in the footnotes will change, becoming more elaborate as you factor in the additional footnotes that correspond with this added material. Furthermore, when you enrich your essay again, this time by examining some, many, or perhaps all of the original texts or primary documents to which those initially helpful secondary sources referred, the pattern of your footnotes will understandably change again, becoming even more elaborate with the inclusion of these corresponding references. The result will be a pattern of footnotes that provides evidence of the deep and wide reading that most examiners find impressive.

Editing

When the draft is completed and the footnotes and bibliography are in order, it is time to complete the final phase of writing an essay, the editing phase, which involves checking for mistakes and making improvements to the expression. Checking for mistakes can be a difficult process because the mind can, with the best intentions, play tricks on us. This is because the mind tends to perceive in terms of schema, a process that can allow it to fill in gaps and correct minor errors in our imaginations so we do not notice them on the page. This means that we can read a grammatically flawed sentence as if it is perfect and not see that, for example, one word had been written twice in a row while another one had been left out altogether. Due to this tendency, if you read the draft quietly to yourself you may overlook several of the mistakes. Your computer's spell-check and grammar-check functions can greatly help you to identify a number of the mistakes that you may have overlooked because it is a programmed machine and not prone to this form of human error. However, because it is a machine it will not exercise the kind of creative judgement that is necessary for effective writing so, despite its virtues, it cannot be relied upon to solve all your editing problems.

In addition to using the computer, there are several less technological methods you can employ to find those illusive remaining errors. It can help if you let the essay sit for a day before you check it. If you look at it with fresh eyes, the mind is less likely to camouflage the problematic grammar or expression. A better way to catch these errors is to read the draft aloud to yourself or, even better, to an obliging a friend or family member. This process will help to highlight the small errors that the mind would have otherwise concealed from you. If other people hear your work, they are better primed to notice any problems because the information in the essay will be fresh to them. An even better approach would be for a friend or family member to read the draft to you. They will be more likely than you would be to read precisely what is on the page rather than what you imagine you wrote. This will allow you to better ascertain whether what you have written is appropriate and effective. Besides, it is very sound practice to have another person check over your work before it is submitted. Academics often do this, usually asking one of their peers to help in this regard. Publishers insist upon this kind of scrutiny, employing professional editors to perform this task. You can do no better than to follow their example and seek assistance.

In addition to catching spelling or grammatical errors, the editing phase is also the ideal time to seek to improve the essay's expression. You may find it opportune to modify some words or sentences, or even rewrite or relocate some sections, so that the language and structure become as effective as you can make them in creating the effects that you intend to generate in your audience. If what you have written works on you, then it may also work on others. If you test the essay on friends and family and it works on them, then it may also work on the audience whom you intend to persuade, your examiner.

The editing phase is also when you make sure that your essay appears to comply with the word length requirements. While on this topic, it should be noted that conciseness is a virtue, as long as it does not compromise clarity. In this regard, you should always seek to make your point with the appropriate amount of words and no more, and you should continually keep this quality in mind while writing the essay, not just during the editing stage. In addition, the ability to write to a particular word length requirement is an important scholarly skill. You should bear in mind that shorter essays are usually that way not because they are substantially more concise in terms of their expression, but rather because they are more summary in their arguments, employing less detail and presenting less evidence. Meanwhile, longer essays cover topics more comprehensively, employing more detail and presenting more evidence, usually derived from more extensive research.

Sometimes word length requirements are set according to a calculation of the complexity and demands of the task or according to the amount of research that students are expected to undertake at different levels in their education, with longer essays required at senior levels more so than at junior levels. However, on other occasions the word length requirements are poorly calculated, or set according to the whim or convenience of educators who may decide out of self-interest to reduce their correction workload. This can produce unrealistic and unfair requirements that can run frustratingly contrary to the demands of the essay question.

Fortunately for students, word length requirements are enforced differently by different examiners. Many examiners will tolerate essays that exceed the limit by about ten per cent before they reprimand students or worse, deduct grades. Some examiners are tolerant of students who exceed the requirement by substantial amounts if their essays are of a very high standard and read well. Some examiners do not mind if students exceed the requirements, particularly if they were not responsible for setting them and, like their students, they too perceive them to be unreasonable. Meanwhile, there are other examiners who may share their students' perception of the unreasonableness of the requirements, yet feel duty bound to enforce them anyway. In addition, many students would have noticed that the enforcement of word length requirements has a curious way of bringing out the tyrannical side of the natures of those examiners who have this predisposition, giving them the opportunity to bully and inflict unnecessary trauma on their classes. The more tolerant and reasonable examiners do not pose a serious problem concerning word length requirements but the others do. Luckily, there are ways of dealing with the issue.

Firstly, you have to become adept at the art of making cuts, which involves passing through several stages of reduction until a suitable number of words is achieved. The first stage involves tightening your sentence construction by cutting out any unnecessary words or by rephrasing some sentences or paragraphs to be more concise. This process has as much to do with producing quality expression as reducing the length of the essay, so it should be carried out regardless of whether the essay needs to be shortened. This fine-tuning usually produces a modest reduction, so if the word length requirement is still exceeded, further measures are required. The next measure is to cut out all the material that is not directly related to your argument, no matter how intrinsically interesting some of it may be. This process produces a leaner more focused work that is often substantially shorter in length. Nevertheless, if you are still short of your objective, you may have to cut out any extra supporting evidence that is important but not essential or even remove some of the less important points in your argument. At this stage, you have gone beyond trimming fat to cutting muscle and bone, which is never a pleasant task. These cuts should be effective in significantly reducing the number of words, but if you are still over the word length requirement you may take this process further until all that remains are the major points and the most important pieces of evidence. At this stage, the cutting process can seem more destructive than productive. So, if you believe that your essay is being ruined because the extent of the cuts is compromising the quality of your work, you may try an alternative approach, subterfuge.

Examiners have neither the time nor the inclination to count the number of words in their students' essays, so they estimate the length of an essay according to its appearance and readability, that is by the number of pages it has compared to the other essays that were submitted and by the degree of time and effort that was required to read it. This means that it is not so much the actual length of the essay that matters but rather its appearance of length. If your work is well written then it will take less time to read and consequently be perceived as shorter than other essays that may have fewer words but are less well written or more complicated. Similarly, if one essay appears to consist of approximately the same number of pages as the other students' essays it will seem to be of about the same number of words. With the formatting functions in your computer you can reduce the margins, line spacing and fonts to magically hide a remarkable number of words that will not be noticed as long as your work is well written and easy to read. Subterfuge may be the only solution if your adherence to unrealistic or unfair word length requirements is forcing you to cut the very material with which you hoped to impress the examiners. Ironically, when students do severely cut their work to meet these requirements they are often not praised for their efforts but rather criticised for what the examiner believed was left out of the argument. Writing to shorter word length requirements is more difficult than writing at length because of the degree of discipline and control that it demands. Cutting can improve the quality of an essay and the ability to trim your work is a valuable skill. However, this process requires judgement. If the cutting that is necessary to meet these requirements reaches a point where it may be counterproductive, then subterfuge may be the only viable alternative.

You will know when the editing process is completed and you are ready to submit the essay, it is when you *feel* ready. This is when the spelling, grammar, expression, structure, and the use of argument and evidence feel just right and you believe that you can do no more to improve your work. You know in your gut that you are ready. But before you submit the essay for assessment, there is one more task to complete. Always make a copy of your work either on a disk or as a photocopy, or both, before you hand it in to your examiner, just in case the submitted copy is lost or destroyed by accident. This means that you can quickly replace it and resubmit if necessary. Furthermore, if you have an extra copy, you are also covered against delays in the assessment and return of any work that you may need for exam preparation.

Essay archetypes: The analytical narrative and the theoretical review

Having discussed the phases of writing an essay in some detail, there are just a couple more facets of essay writing to examine before you are fully versed in what you need to know to excel. The first is essay formats. **There are two different formats, or archetypes, for what we can describe as the standard scholarly essay, and you need to become familiar and adept at using both, the analytical narrative and the theoretical review.** The analytical narrative is preferred at high school level and appreciated at university, while the theoretical review is almost totally absent at the high school level and increasingly fashionable at universities largely due to the prevalence of (predominantly left-wing or politically correct) theory, so much so that it is displacing the analytical narrative in many faculties. If students are unfamiliar with these formats and they employ one of them when they need to employ the other, they may unexpectedly find themselves disappointing certain examiners whom they expected to impress or experiencing demoralising difficulties in making the transition from high school to university.

The analytical narrative format is more empirical than the other format, which means that it is more interested in employing facts as evidence to answer questions. This evidence is extracted from sources, either primary or secondary, and arranged in the form of an argument that often simultaneously tells a story as it analyses and explains each facet of the topic. Put simply, to answer a question the essay tells a story that analyses as it progresses, or it analyses a topic primarily (but not exclusively) by compiling, presenting and interpreting facts. Even though the insights or perspectives of various relevant authors in the field may be referred to, greater attention is given to the presentation of empirical evidence.

With the theoretical review format, the student approaches a question by critically drawing upon and assembling in the form of an argument the theories or insights of others. The evidence used to provide the answer is primarily these theories and insights. For example, the argument might consist of Foucault supported by Derrida and complemented by Barthes. Even when empirical or factual evidence is employed, it is treated in the same fashion that theoretical material is treated. Instead of simply presenting the empirical or factual evidence in the essay and acknowledging the source in a footnote, when writing in this essay format the student would instead refer to the implications of the empirical research of such and such an author, who is named and discussed in the essay as if he were a theorist. For example, the empirical research conducted by Anderson into absolutism can be seen to lend considerable support to Marx's theory of social development.

If, for example, an assignment asked students to assess the value of a particular theory, an essay written according to the format of the analytical narrative would assess the theory's value in the light of evidence that was extracted from relevant sources, which, of course, were produced by various authors who were acknowledged in the footnotes. Meanwhile, an essay written in the format of the theoretical review would assess the theory in the light of the interpretations and findings of these relevant authors who were named and discussed in the body of the essay. For students who understand the differences between these formats, shifting from one to the other is not that difficult. This is because it usually involves treating the same sources in marginally different ways, either by giving emphasis to the evidence provided by an author or by giving emphasis to the insight of an author that was based on certain evidence.

Some essays may combine both formats and this can be quite effective. Nevertheless, students should be aware that many academics consider the approach employed in the theoretical review format to be worthier and they are more likely to reward essays that are written in this manner. Meanwhile, most high school teachers are generally more comfortable with essays written in the analytical narrative format, so students who have been rewarded for producing that kind of essay at school need to be prepared to modify their approach when they make the transition from school to university so they can continue to be highly rewarded.

Style: Using scholarly English

Having noted the formats in which you can be expected to write an essay, it is appropriate to deal with another important dimension of essay writing – style. **The style of writing that you use to present your argument can have a profound effect on the way in which your argument is appreciated and assessed, even though style generally has little to do with the content of your argument.** There are therefore great advantages for students who develop an effective command of writing style.

The style of writing that it is necessary for students to become adept at using is scholarly English, which is the style of learned prose found in academic books and journals. This form of English is generally appreciated as the style of writing that is most commonly associated with the expression of intelligent ideas. Scholarly English obeys the conventions of formal English and it is comfortable using the technical terminology associated with the subject being discussed. It also follows a number of time-honoured stylistic conventions of its own, to which students are expected to conform. Scholarly English tends to avoid emotive or colloquial language, except on very rare occasions when they may be employed to make a point notably interesting or dramatic. Generally, it employs a tone that is moderate, reasoned, disciplined and qualified in its responses, claiming to conclude only what the evidence implies and no more. According to academic convention, this restraint is expected to be particularly evident when criticising the work of other scholars. In addition, modesty is preferred, especially at university level, when presenting your findings or conclusions, even if they are significant. Nevertheless, you may have noticed that at high school level, adherence to these scholarly conventions is appreciated but is more relaxed in practice and essays can be, for example, more assertive. This is partly because the application of academic standards at high school is not as stringent due to the lower expectations placed on high school students compared to those at university. However, it is also partly due to the tendency of most teachers to deal far less with the writing found in academic books and journals than most academics do, so many teachers are consequently less attuned to these conventions than academics. In addition, teachers also tend to be more comfortable and familiar with the products of broadsheet journalism and this has subtly affected these teachers' understanding of what constitutes scholarly writing.

For most scholarly writing you have a choice between predominantly using either the past or present tense, each of which creates a different effect. If you write mostly using the past tense (for example: 'Plato said…'), it lends the work a quality of being resolved, completed and solid. By contrast, if you write in the present tense (for example: 'Plato says…'), it conveys a greater sense of immediacy, relevance and fluidity. In terms of common sense, it makes more sense to write mostly in the past tense because most of the subject matter discussed occurred in the past. Nevertheless, it is acceptable to comment as if the text of an author, even an ancient author like Plato, maintains a dialogue with the public, for example: 'Plato argues…' Generally, the past tense is to be preferred because it can give the impression of finality to your argument that can add an aura of authority to your writing and conclusions that subtly works in your favour. Nevertheless, different educators will have different preferences in this regard, so if you discover that your examiner prefers the use of the present tense, use that tense for work to be assessed by that examiner.

Style: From competence to mastery

The development of your scholarly writing style from competence to mastery can progress through three phases, from appreciating and applying several very profitable basic concepts and skills through to an intermediate level of control over different forms of language and then on to a very sophisticated command over the nature of communication. Even though the basic and intermediate levels of skill are sufficient for you to consistently produce work with a high standard of merit, which can provide a foundation for consistently achieving high grades, I shall also share with you some very powerful advanced techniques of writing that can dramatically improve your persuasive ability, even if you only attain an imperfect grasp of them. But first, let's start with the basics.

The principle to adopt that will provide you with the quickest path to an effective writing style is to simply write to be understood, using clarity and simplicity as your guiding criteria. This involves saying what you have to say clearly. Scholarly language may sometimes have to deal with complex ideas but it does not itself have to be complex. Avoid assuming that your educator is an expert who would become impatient if you spelt out things clearly. The opposite attitude is more likely, with educators, like most readers, tending to appreciate writing that is easy to read. When writing, it is more profitable for you to assume that your audience is ignorant and requires you to explain things clearly. This attitude will discourage students from writing in an annoyingly abridged style that seems to have resulted from being intimidated by the perception that they are writing for an expert who does not need to have things explained. In regards to your vocabulary, chose the *right* word to say precisely what you mean rather than big or obscure words that are often self-consciously chosen in an attempt to convey a sense of intelligence rather than to communicate effectively. In addition, avoid the overuse of pronouns, acronyms, abbreviations or anything else that may force the reader to interrupt the flow of their reading experience to ponder the meaning of a term. Examiners are human, and just like you they appreciate an easy enjoyable read. **Keep it simple. Keep it clear. If you use language that is readily understood, you will be readily understood.**

If you adopt the principle of writing to be understood, and use the guiding criteria of simplicity and clarity, you will find the quality and effectiveness of your writing will significantly improve. Once you feel comfortable with this basic yet very effective writing style, you can build upon it by expanding your repertoire to progress to the intermediate stage, where you can vary your style to suit the particular tastes of different examiners. The benefits of this stylistic flexibility have been discussed earlier, in the second chapter of this book that included a discussion of the benefits of tuning into your examiner's preferred forms of language and reflecting that form of language in your own writing. This task is not as daunting as some students assume. It is primarily a question of harnessing and cultivating a skill that you already have and exercise often, virtually every day, and applying it to essay writing. For example, you would comfortably use one form of language to talk to young children and another to talk to adults. Similarly, you can already shift effortlessly from using one style of language when you are talking with friends in the school or campus grounds to another when you are in class and the educator is present. There are times when writing or speaking that you would have, for example, expressed yourself precisely, while at other times you provided extensive detail. The skill of stylistic flexibility simply involves determining whether your examiner prefers either precise or detailed or any other form of expression and adjusting your style to suit the circumstances. Even though I have stressed the value of simplicity and clarity, you would be aware that because there are some examiners who prefer big or pretentious words, there are occasions when you may see the need to skilfully sacrifice some of your linguistic simplicity and clarity to achieve a more favourable response from these examiners. Nevertheless, in cases like these, while you may for tactical reasons sacrifice some simplicity and clarity in your vocabulary, you would preserve these qualities in the structure of the essay. Your stylistic flexibility should be built upon a foundation of the qualities of simplicity and clarity, significantly complementing them rather than substantially compromising them.

Harnessing the power of language

A progression from the intermediate stage to a mastery of writing is facilitated by a more profound understanding of how the mind perceives language and why it shifts our emotions. Even though what I have already taught you is sufficient to consistently deliver high grades and effectively handle a multitude of situations in which you may find yourself, these additional sophisticated concepts and techniques can enable you to take your skills a step further, to a level of merit beyond 'A+', to mastery. When you have this understanding, which I am about to share with you, you will be able to cleverly manipulate with a remarkable degree of control the responses of your audience, who are, in terms of your essay writing, your examiners. This degree of awareness, which will be new to many of you, can be factored into your writing to make your language dramatically even more persuasive.

Firstly, we must recognise that the mind is not as rational as our egos would like it to be, and emotion plays a greater role in how people appreciate arguments than many people acknowledge. This is evident in how the mind perceives language. This psychological phenomenon can be appreciated if we examine two sentences that from a rational perspective say virtually the same thing yet use different words and consequently leave contrasting emotional impressions on the audience:

I will not disappoint you.
I will help you succeed.

Say each of the above sentences to yourself and while doing so pay attention to your emotional response. At a rational level of thinking, about which we are fully conscious, the message of the first sentence (I will not disappoint you) is positive; yet at another deeper emotional level of thinking, about which we are far less conscious, this sentence arouses noticeable feelings that are negative. Having directed yourself to think carefully about the feelings that language can generate as it is interpreted and understood, you would have noticed the discontinuity between the way the first sentence is appreciated at different levels of consciousness, which can in turn affect its persuasiveness. Meanwhile, the meaning of the second sentence (I will help you succeed) is appreciated as positive at both levels of thinking, rationally and emotionally, with its emotional meaning being positive to the point of being uplifting.

Why do these sentences convey approximately the same meaning at one level yet at a deeper subconscious emotional level create distinctively different impressions? This is because the message of the first sentence is positive yet the key words used to express its positive message are emotionally negative. The word 'disappoint', as it is processed and understood, leaves a negative impression. This is because the mind, to understand many words, has to, in a sense, experience or re-experience the meaning of the word. The word 'disappoint' was learnt and understood as being associated with corresponding negative feelings and at the emotional level it is appreciated in this negative fashion despite the presence of the qualifying term 'not' that is intended to remove the negativity of the word 'disappoint', a qualifying term that is noticed at the rational level of thinking but barely noticed at the deeper subconscious emotional level. On the other hand, the second sentence (I will help you succeed) uses positive words like 'succeed'. As the mind processes this word and understands it, it experiences the positive feelings associated with this word, which are affirming, reassuring and even inspiring. **In a very real sense, many words are appreciated as feelings, being felt in order to be understood. Now that you understand this, you can begin to use language to generate precisely the feelings in your audience that you wish to generate.** This is because to understand what you are saying they will have to experience certain emotions associated with particular words. This psychological process, of course, happens all the time whether we choose to acknowledge it or not. However, when we do appreciate this phenomenon, we can reorient and train ourselves to use it to our advantage.

When you are writing essays or any other piece of writing that is intended to persuade your audience, such as a job application or an excuse letter, you need to be aware of the feelings associated with words and their meanings. For example, in a job application letter there should be no language used that to be understood generates negative emotions in the reader. If an applicant expresses positive ideas using negative language, his audience will appreciate his positive message with their conscious mind but their subconscious will generate an uneasy feeling. They may come away from reading the applicant's language aware that the letter said all the right things but for some reason that they cannot pinpoint they just have an uneasy feeling about this candidate. But if the applicant had expressed his positive message using language that is associated with positive feelings, then the application letter would have been more likely to have generated positive feelings in the reader and consequently been perceived to stand out from its competitors even though several other letters may have also said all the right things.

When writing an essay, you need to bear in mind that, for example, the term 'not disappoint' is appreciated differently to 'succeed'. Keep in mind the emotions that you want to generate in your audience and choose words that complement rather than contradict your intentions. You may have to think about the meanings of words more profoundly and comprehensively than you have done in the past, to look beyond the dictionary definitions of words to appreciate their potential emotional impact. Your efforts will be worthwhile because when you become practiced at using language to generate the emotions in your audience that are conducive to effective persuasion, then you would have become formidable indeed, able to manipulate favourable responses virtually at will.

Harnessing the power of structure

In addition to understanding the nature of the comprehension of meaning in language and the generation of corresponding emotions, there is another dimension to mastering the art of writing that is necessary to discuss, the impact of structure. We have previously talked about structure, which is the sequence in which you present your material, in terms of logic and the formal structure of essays. Now I intend to introduce you to another way of appreciating this dimension of writing that will increase your persuasiveness even further. To do this, I have to take you into a deeper understanding of the nature of art and how it is appreciated. We will begin with the following insightful principle: **Works of art are a series of ideas presented in a sequence that is ultimately intended to produce an emotional response.** This is the case with writing, as well as with music, cinema and theatre. It is also the case with painting, photography, sculpture and architecture, even though the sequence in which you experience the ideas expressed in these works of art may vary according to the angle from which you view and therefore read the image or object. It is also the case with works that may seem, at face value, to be designed to appeal exclusively to rational faculties. I suggest that a total absence of any emotional response is impossible, because even when dealing with something as apparently dry as a formula in physics we may experience, for example, satisfaction in our ability to understand the formula, along with feelings of appreciation for the enlightenment that the formula provides. For art to be effective in making an impression on us, it needs to leave us in a different emotional state to the one that existed in us before we experienced the work of art or serve to perpetuate an emotional state that we sought to continue. We recognise this quality, unconsciously, when we praise a work of art for having been 'moving'. We also recognise it, unconsciously again, when we contemplate watching a film and declare that we could do with a comedy tonight. This means that we want to experience a work of art that will present us with a sequence of ideas that will shift us from the emotional state that we are currently in, to the one that we desire – amusement. Some artworks are even classified according to genres that are named after the emotions that they are intended to generate, such as horror, suspense, thriller or romance. Even though you may not have thought about art in this fashion before, but rather simply responded to it, if you pause and reflect on what this principle implies you will soon appreciate that it begins to explain much about how and why you respond to works of art in the ways that you do.

Let us further examine this revealing principle about the nature of art. The sequence in which you experience the ideas in a work of art is crucial to how you will appreciate it. This is because the preceding ideas can influence how the following ideas are perceived or, put another way, one piece of information can affect how the next piece of information is understood. This point can be illustrated in the following fashion. Imagine that you are watching a film. You are presented with a scene depicting a woman who walks into a bedroom and, with her back to the cupboard, proceeds to make the bed. Understandably, this scene would be perceived as mundane if not boring. But imagine if the previous scene had depicted a sinister intruder who climbed into the bedroom through the window then concealed himself in the cupboard to peer ominously through the louvres in the cupboard door. Then imagine that you see the original scene again, where a woman walks into the bedroom and, with her back to the cupboard, proceeds to make the bed. This new piece of information completely changes how the original scene is perceived. Instead of being mundane and boring, it becomes chillingly suspenseful even though nothing in the scene has changed. What has changed is that the audience has been given a preceding piece of information that changes their perception of the scene that followed.

This awareness of the importance of the sequence in which ideas are presented is meant to encourage you to appreciate how a manipulation of the sequence can be a means to create the desired effect in an audience. What is especially pleasing about this process is that the writer can surreptitiously manipulate the emotional responses of the audience in a fashion that makes the audience believe that they are in command of their thoughts and how they reach their conclusions on the subject matter, when it is actually the writer who is feeding them the material with which they make their calculations. This material being, of course, crafted to encourage the audience to think in a certain direction. What is particularly valuable about this technique is not only its effectiveness but also its invisibility. It is particularly suited to helping those who seek to introduce radical new ideas in the face of a potentially hostile academic establishment. This is because it allows the readers to believe that they reached the radical conclusion of their own accord, therefore feeling as if they own this conclusion rather than resentfully thinking that they have been pushed towards it by a precocious writer. So rather than go down the perilous path of openly undermining the credibility of a widely respected member of the academic establishment for basing his theory on highly problematic premises, you can instead tactfully show the implications of your new material for the premises of his argument, and then deliberately pull your punch. So instead of crystallising the implications of your findings in a hard-hitting conclusion that may antagonise the members of the academic establishment whom you seek to win over, you allow your readers to use your material to see that academic's theory in a new light and draw the obvious conclusion for themselves. The effect is the same as in the cinematic example that I provided earlier. Although you present that academic's theory in a balanced matter-of-fact manner, you have preceded this statement with information that leads your readers to look at that theory in a different, more critical light. In this fashion, a writer can avoid appearing confrontational and thereby significantly increase his chances of winning acceptance for radically new ideas.

In order to be used effectively, there is another dimension to this advanced writing technique that needs to be factored into your calculations. While it is the case that art is appreciated as a sequence of ideas, one must also bear in mind that the audience brings to their experience of the work of art their biases, that is their ideologies, values, ethics etc. Consequently, they may factor in their own contributions to the sequence drawn from their own ideas, knowledge and experiences, adding or sometimes subtracting elements from that sequence. This may be done inadvertently, by misunderstanding some of the ideas so they do not figure in their appreciation of the artwork, or by becoming so inspired that they find themselves relating to the artwork in such a personal way that they impute their own thoughts on the subject into their experience of the artwork. This is due to the fact that when we read, view or listen to a work of art, this is usually an intellectually active rather than passive process. Often the work of art will generate relevant thoughts and recollections that are inserted into the sequence of ideas that personalise the experience of that work of art for that individual to perhaps lead them to see a different meaning to the one intended by the author. For example, the impact of bias may lead one person to view documentary war footage as a testimony to human courage and another to see it as depicting man's inhumanity to man. Different people can respond differently to the same stimulus. Many writers erroneously expect to take a broad spectrum of readers and feed them down a funnel so they all come out thinking and feeling the same. This cannot be achieved to the extent that most writers hope and expect, so much so that it should not even be attempted. Having said this, it is the case that if you know the biases of your audience you can factor them into your calculations. People view works of art through their paradigms or frameworks of understanding so that the information they receive is filtered by their ideology and values. If the creator of a work of art understands the ideology and values of each segment of his overall audience, he can include information that can manipulate the responses of each segment and thereby achieve greater control over their emotional responses. It is even possible to simultaneously cultivate the positive responses of, for example, diametrically opposed left and right-wing audience segments, provided that you provide sufficient material to stimulate positive responses for each segment that is also carefully crafted to avoid antagonising the other segment, a process that requires some skill.

Most people have a tendency to see what they want or expect to see, and they prefer to see material that reinforces their beliefs and to downplay or avoid material that challenges them. If you express yourself tactfully and avoid the use of value-laden words that suggest bias, you can allow the members of each audience segment to highlight in their own imaginations what appeals to them in your work and to brush over the material that they find less appealing or unappealing. It is therefore possible to weave, for example, pro-left and pro-right-wing statements and findings together in a fashion that allows the left-wing people to focus on the left-wing material and the right-wing people to focus on the right-wing material, so that the members of each audience segment come away believing that although you acknowledged some of the 'merits' of the opposite side, ultimately you supported their position and you are on their side. While it is unlikely that you will have each of your audience segments thinking the same way about your work, you can make it far more likely that their responses are predominantly positive, although each segment would have experienced a positive response for different reasons.

A word of caution, although these techniques are powerful due to their subtlety they are also vulnerable due to their subtlety. They are only effective if you have established an advantageous context in which you and your work will be interpreted. They will not work if the student, writer or artist has already established a profile or reputation for being associated with a political party, interest group or partisan position, especially if it is contrary to the beliefs of the principal people whom you seek to impress. This perception will usually override any of the deliberate ambiguity that you may seek to impute into the interpretation of your work. Nevertheless, it is possible to shape or reshape the context in which you and your work will be interpreted and perceived. This process has already been discussed in the second chapter of this book when I explained the benefits that result from establishing for oneself the kind of persona that educators like to reward, such as that of the keen, diligent, capable student or of the 'chip off the old block'. To the elements of those personas, I would like to add the powerful ingredients of goodwill as well as an appreciation of balance and fairness.

One of the most powerful resources you can employ when seeking to persuade people, including potentially uncooperative or hostile people, is goodwill. This is because it is extremely difficult to be unfair to someone who exudes goodwill towards others. It is therefore extremely advantageous for you to exude a positive enthusiastic attitude that is both infectious and endearing. Secondly, although the qualities of balance and fairness have their own intrinsic worth in promoting good scholarship, they are also powerful weapons to employ in your efforts to persuade. If you are concerned that there is a chance that you and your work may not be treated fairly, especially by those in authority over you, then you should seek to treat others fairly, especially those who are in authority over you, and make it well known to them that you value the qualities of balance and fairness very highly. Even the most biased authorities do not like to think of themselves as biased but rather as people who value balance and fairness, so by associating yourself closely with these principles you can create a formidable moral obstacle in the conscience of those people who may have the potential to act unfairly towards you. If you treat others how you would like to be treated, you stand a greater chance of bringing out the better sides of their natures and creating an advantageous context in which you and your work will be perceived.

While an awareness of these advanced techniques and the principles behind them can be helpful for all students, most high school and undergraduate university students will probably be content to consistently generate high grades by achieving a sufficient degree of merit and by mimicking the bias of their examiners, taking care to avoid the dangers that can arise out of producing original and potentially controversial work. These advanced techniques were designed primarily to help those postgraduate students who have developed radically new and original ideas and who intend to publish their findings and be rewarded for their efforts rather than face marginalisation or vilification by members of an academic establishment wedded to opposing beliefs. In addition, these techniques also have a wider application than achieving success in the education system. They may be employed by any new writer or artist who has radical potentially controversial ideas and who seeks acceptance for their work and to avoid the hazards that can result from challenging the potentially hostile custodians of the status quo.

Now that we have acquired a profound and comprehensive insight into the writing of a standard scholarly essay, it is appropriate that we turn our attention to mastering other tasks that students are expected to perform.

Becoming even more accomplished: The art of creative writing, the analysis of literature, poetry analysis, literature reviews, research reports, essays for vocational courses, problem-solving exercises, public speaking, and course or job applications

Creative writing

Although creative writing is more versatile than the standard scholarly argumentative essay, it has more in common with it than many students appreciate, and these similarities are instructive. Consequently, what you have already learnt about producing quality argumentative essays is just as relevant to producing quality creative essays.

First, let us recap a relevant point that was made earlier while we were learning the art of essay writing. We noted the following: **Although some creative writing can be unorthodox or experimental, it can generally** be appreciated that for creative writing to be valued as literature it must have something to say about the nature of the world or the human condition. So, just like the argumentative essay, the creative essay has something to say, only it makes most of its points in a different fashion. Instead of making its points directly, as would be the case in an argumentative essay that systematically presents reason and evidence, creative writing makes most of its points indirectly by creating characters, situations and settings that imply these points.

With creative writing, your choice of a topic is crucial to your success. I estimate that it is responsible for about 50 per cent or more of the grade, so give this matter careful consideration because it can be decisive. A good writer understands his audience, and for you the audience is your examiner. If you pick a topic that appeals to your examiner or, better still, touches your examiner personally, you have given yourself a major head start. Ideally, you should choose a topic that also inspires you, so you can write with enthusiasm. The topic should also be suited to the time and space that is available. For relatively short essays, often it is best to write about a small incident that can be milked for its meaning or choose an aspect of a multifaceted topic, like family relationships, rather than attempt to engage with the subject matter comprehensively. In addition, even though you may be writing fiction, you can often write more believable stories if you base them on real incidents, observations or sentiments. It is far easier to write well about subjects that you know well.

At this point it is also opportune to remind ourselves of another important principle that we learnt that can guide us during the creative writing process: Works of art are a series of ideas presented in a sequence that is ultimately intended to produce an emotional response. In this context, stories can be seen as having two elements. There is a narrative element that describes things, events, and how a character gets from point A to point B. There is also an emotional element that evokes sentiments in the audience. It is this emotional element that has the most literary power and it is what you need to emphasise if your story is to have maximum impact. Therefore, focus on evoking feelings rather than the practical aspects of the narrative. Think of the narrative element as a means to an end, and handle it economically. Therefore, if your topic is the bond between a grandfather and his grandson, and the scene that you devised to express this idea is of a young man who visits his ailing grandfather to seize the opportunity to tell him that he loves him, then be very brief in describing how the grandson arrived at his grandfather's home. Instead, devote your attention to describing the emotional poignancy of the moment.

For those of you who are not used to writing to evoke feelings in your audience, here is how to do it. To move your audience emotionally, what you have to do is describe emotion accurately. The key word is accurately. If the story is told, for example, in the first person, it is not sufficient to simply say 'When I visited my sick grandfather I felt sad'. Instead, detail these feelings precisely. This can involve describing the thoughts, actions, or sensations that may coincide with experiencing certain feelings. Here is an example:

> Young men are notoriously reticent about showing their emotions, and I was no different. As I stood by grandfather's sickbed, I froze, struck silent by the enormity of the feelings I had at that moment. Then, forcing myself, I uncharacteristically embraced my grandfather. 'I love you Granddad', I told him, with my face near his ear. My voice cracked as I said it. 'I love you too', was his reply. A tear ran helplessly down my cheek. Luckily, I was not facing him and he did not see it.

In this passage, I have accurately described an emotional moment. The scene includes sentimental details that many people would overlook, yet their inclusion provides most of the emotional impact. I encourage you to think carefully about emotional subject matter and to find the words to accurately describe it. The more that you practise, the better you will become. As we have already noted, many words are appreciated as feelings, being felt in order to be understood. The words that you use to accurately describe, for example, family love, can evoke these sentiments because to understand the words that you use your audience will have to re-experience these emotions. In addition, an accurate description of the emotional dimension of a scene is likely to encourage readers to recall similar incidents in their own lives and re-experience the feelings associated with these incidents. If you were moved by that passage, these are the techniques that I employed to do it, and with these techniques, you can do it too.

Your brainstorming and/or research will determine what you want to say about your topic and how you can express these points as characters, situations, and settings. This is when your imagination should run freely. Nevertheless, when it comes to selecting the material to use in the essay, maintain your focus to only include what communicates your message, otherwise you can create confusion when your audience (your examiner) interprets the story. When you plan your creative writing essay, bear in mind the versatility of the medium. You may choose to include an introduction, body and conclusion, as required in the standard scholarly essay, or you may choose to, for example, skip the introductory material to go straight into the action, commencing the story telling at an enticingly dramatic moment. Despite the opportunity for versatility, do not forget that because creative writing has something to say, there needs to be a conclusion or climactic point where the meaning of the story is crystallised.

While on the topic of creative essays, it should be recognised that there are forms of non-fictional writing that students may be required to produce that vary from formally structured scholarly essays, such as pieces written in journalistic and other less-academic styles. These forms of writing can employ various stylistic elements to enhance their appeal. In addition to the option of starting the story at a dramatic moment, these pieces may open with an intriguing or revealing anecdote to generate curiosity, or present an attention-grabbing statistic or an alarming reference to a controversy to spark interest, or they may open by evoking an atmosphere or mood conducive to the appreciation of the message of the story, or they may provide references that enhance the human interest qualities of the writing so the audience can vividly relate to the subject matter. Of course, these elements can be employed in the opening or at other opportune moments. Nevertheless, when using any of these stylistic elements, or others, keep in mind that their value is enhanced by the way they serve the purpose of the piece or support its contention.

Many students do not believe that you can prepare for the creative essays encountered in tests or exams because they do not know what the topics will be and have no way of guessing them. This is not the case. You can effectively prepare for writing creative essays under test or exam conditions because most of the topics are not topics at all but rather non-specific prompts that can be interpreted in almost any fashion. They may include phrases such as 'a perfect day', 'an eerie experience', or 'a favourite person', or photographic prompts like a trail of footprints in the sand. The trick with these photographic prompts is to interpret them metaphorically, so the trail of footprints becomes defined as, for example, life's journey, which is an easier subject about which to write. Other frequently recurring essay topics are related to thematic subjects. Once you know them, you know what to expect. Here are some that I have seen often: friendship, family love, relationships, identity, childhood, coming of age, the generation gap, the value of education, ambition, success, happiness, power, justice, freedom, tolerance, the nature of the modern world, progress, and the future. These are subjects that most people would be expected to have reflected upon and have opinions. They draw on your general knowledge, to which you should be adding all the time. At this point, you may have noticed that all the non-specific prompts can easily be related to these thematic subjects, so you can use these prompts to write about the thematic subject of your choice. Meanwhile, any specific issues that may be put forward as topics should also be familiar because they are usually drawn from the agenda of the dominant ideology within the education system; currently it is political correctness. These topics can include war and violence, pollution, censorship, women's liberation, racism, poverty, bioethics, and so on. By now, you would have recognised that there are definite patterns regarding what to expect. It follows that once you know them you can prepare in advance. It may help you to spend some time, before the test or exam, brainstorming to organise your thoughts on the typical thematic subjects so you can write about them at short notice. When you do so, make sure that your material includes some philosophical ideas that address the complexities of the subject as well as other material that can evoke emotional responses in the audience. Above all, remember that if you want to succeed, this material should reflect the examiner's bias.

    You may not yet realise it but now that you understand the process of creative writing, you are also substantially better equipped to perform literary analysis, a task that many students and teachers find difficult, although these teachers are usually reluctant to admit this to their classes. As you already know, an argumentative essay makes its points directly by employing reason and evidence. Creative writing begins with the author's purpose, this being the points the author wishes to make in the form of an argument. These points are then made indirectly through the creation of characters situations and settings that imply these points. Literary analysis simply reverses the process involved in creative writing. It decodes the characters, situations and settings to reveal the underlying points and argument, and hence the meaning of the text. Creative writing and literary analysis complement each other with an instructively revealing symmetry. Because each process is the reverse of the other, the more practice you have with one the better you can become at the other.

Literary analysis

The ability to capture the meaning of a text in a few words, sentences or paragraphs (depending on its complexity) is a valuable skill that takes time and practice to develop, which once attained should be continually refined throughout your life. Although many students initially appreciate this skill as being related to studying English literature, its beneficial applications are numerous, ranging from understanding novels, history books, newspaper articles, legal documents and scientific publications, to enriching your enjoyment of films and television programs. This skill is one of the hallmarks of an educated person. I became acutely aware of its value when I was an undergraduate student at university and I observed the way many academics could impressively encapsulate the meaning of texts in a few sentences. I realised that I too needed to acquire that skill. In pursuit of this objective, and after much reflection and practice, I came up with the following guidelines.

With literary analysis, there are several principles you should bear in mind to improve your skill. Firstly, remember to treat the text as the creation of an author (or authors) to serve a purpose. Among other things, this approach will prevent students from falling into the trap of discussing fictional characters as if they are real people rather than the products of someone's imagination, an easy mistake that many teachers also make. It will also help to prevent students from falling into the trap of projecting their own ideas into the meaning of the text when they may not be relevant, a mistake that many people often make. This disciplined attitude ensures that you approach the text with an analytical frame of mind that is conducive to comprehending its meaning.

Secondly, when seeking to understand a text, there are two interrelated questions to ask: what the author says and how the author says it. The first question (what the author says) is about clarifying the meanings or messages of the text, usually referred to as the themes. All texts contain main themes, which are the main messages that run consistently through the text. Most texts also contain sub-themes, which are minor messages found running through the text or sections of it. These themes constitute the meaning of the text or the author's purpose. **When you have defined the major and minor themes, you have found the magic key that can unlock the meaning of every part of the text.** The second question (how the author says it) refers to how various expressive devices were used to convey these messages, such as through the creation of characters, situations, settings, as well as with the construction of the plot and the use of language. With films, this would also include cinematography, composition, performance, staging, costumes, editing, lighting, sound and music. The most important of these two interrelated questions is the first, because the meaning of the text is relevant to every essay question that you can be asked. Even if the question focused on one expressive device, such as a character, you can only effectively answer this question by discussing the role this character plays in communicating the themes. Every question at some stage comes back to the themes, so if you get them right, you can get everything else right.

How does one determine the themes or the meaning of a text? If the author of a text is an effective communicator, then the meaning or themes should emanate directly from reading the text. So, when you read it be prepared to appreciate the obvious. However, in many cases the meanings, or rather a more profound and precise appreciation of the meanings, can seem less than obvious. To detect these requires background knowledge related to two contexts, that in which the author wrote and that in which the text is set. Your general knowledge may be sufficient to help you to understand a number of texts, but if it falls short, some research is required. You need to learn about the biography of the author to determine the author's preoccupations, beliefs, values and interests that were reflected in their work. You also need to learn about the events and issues at the time the author wrote that might have influenced their work, as well as their relationship to any trends or movements within the artistic, literary or academic communities. This information will alert you to what to look for in the text to determine its meaning. In addition, it helps to become reasonably knowledgeable about the period in which the text is set, such as during the Vietnam War, because particular settings can be appreciated as more conducive to communicating certain messages than others. For example, you may have noticed that writers or film-makers who seek to convey patriotic messages often prefer the Second World War as a setting, while those with anti-war messages often prefer the Vietnam War.

Luckily, for many students of English literature this task is made easier by the availability of published study notes on a wide range of texts. If you read one or more of these booklets before you read the text, you will be more likely to come to the text as an informed reader who has a greater awareness of what he is looking for. Before you commence, I offer a word of warning. These study notes can vary dramatically in terms of their quality. Some of them are so insightful that reading the actual text afterwards may seem unnecessary. These are usually written by highly qualified experts, usually with doctorates, and their analysis will have a noticeably authoritative quality about it. Meanwhile, other study notes are of a poor standard, with some being flawed to the point of being scandalously misleading. These are usually written by high school teachers who are seeking to earn extra money after hours. While the qualifications of the author of the study notes is often a guide to their value, it should be recognised that sometimes some highly qualified scholars can run off on some theoretically inspired tangent and miss the main point of the text, while some study notes produced by teachers are competent and informative. These variations in quality suggest that the safest approach to orientating yourself towards a text is to explore a range of study notes. After this background research, when reading the text you should take many notes as you proceed to ensure that you consolidate your understanding and command over the significant material. When you have completed this research, organise the material so that it begins with a clear and succinct statement of the main themes and sub-themes, followed by a more detailed discussion of this material. This should provide you with the resources to answer any essay question that you may be asked.

If there are no published study notes available, there are other resources you can access, such as biographical materials regarding the author, studies of the periods in which the author wrote or wrote about, as well as material covering intellectual trends that may have affected the author. If your knowledge is limited, this research can be time-consuming. Nevertheless, the more research of this kind that you undertake, the more knowledgeable you will become and you may as a result become so knowledgeable about, for example, the radical politics of the 1960s, that when you encounter texts from this period, or about it, you are primed to understand them immediately.

The analysis of texts required at a high school level usually stops at the point of understanding what the author says and how the author says it, but at university this analysis can go a step farther by asking students to examine a text from a particular theoretical perspective, such as feminism or post-colonialism. This requires students to do another round of research to clarify this theoretical perspective so it is applied appropriately to the text. For example, a post-colonial analysis may require a student to look at a text in terms of its relationship to the legacy of colonialism, especially its conscious or unconscious justification for the unequal power relationships between the races, or between the Western and other civilisations. This may involve looking at the text in terms of implied meanings or discourses that were not intended by the author. Nevertheless, it will help students to conduct these forms of analysis more effectively if they begin with a clear understanding of what the author did intend to say, which can keep their theoretical analysis grounded.

On most occasions, students are expected to demonstrate their understanding of a text in an analytical essay, but sometimes students are presented with the option of writing a creative response, where they produce, for example, a postscript or prequel to a novel or provide additional material that adds depth to a character, tasks that should be completed in the writing style of the author being studied. Although some students who doubt their analytical abilities may see this response as an easier option, they should think again. The creative response requires twice as much work as an analytical essay. Furthermore, instead of being avoidable, a sound analysis of the text is inescapable when completing this option. Students have to firstly determine what the author said and how the author said it, so that their creative response begins from a solid foundation. They then apply this knowledge to produce a credible addition to the novelist's story that is thematically and stylistically consistent. Although a creative response can be an educationally rewarding experience, students seeking an easier option should perhaps think again.

Poetry analysis

Now that you have a greater understanding of literary analysis, we can turn to the demanding problem of poetry analysis, which is arguably the most difficult and potentially stressful task that students are asked to undertake. To be frank, although some poetry can be a delight, much of it is an ordeal because it is so difficult to decipher. At its best, poetry can be a condensed, sometimes lyrical form of writing that can be richly layered in meaning. It often requires from the readers extra effort to fully unravel these meanings, a process that can be a rewarding experience. On the other hand, poetry can degenerate into a seemingly pointless pretentious form of intellectual game playing with the audience, where the poet balks at the idea of stating something plainly in favour of burying the meaning in cryptic puzzles that challenge the readers to unravel them. After expending great effort to determine what the poet had to say, one can be left with a profound sense of disappointment, 'Is that all there is!'

As with literary analysis, in poetry analysis students have to answer two interrelated questions, what the author says and how the author says it. Although poetry analysis requires considerable attention to be devoted to the second question, involving explaining the application of expressive poetic techniques, it is not possible to effectively deal with this dimension until the first question is answered, so that is where your analysis commences.

Many students can read a poem for the first time and come away with little or no idea what it means. Do not worry. This is normal. Do not be hard on yourself. It is only the first step in stage one of the process of analysis. You should recognise that it is almost impossible to successfully interpret a poem without background knowledge on the poet. When you learn about the poet's preoccupations, beliefs, values and interests you may begin to notice some of them reflected in the poem being studied.

In addition, when you learn about the significant events and issues at the time the poet wrote, as well as the poet's relationship to any trends or movements within the artistic, literary or academic communities, you may begin to see these influences reflected in the content of the poem. Furthermore, if your general knowledge is insufficient, it can also be illuminating to become briefed regarding the period in which the poem is set, or on the subject matter or issues with which the poem is supposed to deal. At last, with this background knowledge, the meaning should be becoming clearer. After this research, read the poem again, and keep re-reading and reflecting on it until its meaning is fully understood. When you have determined the meaning of the poem, you have completed the first stage of the analysis. Now that you know what the poet said, you can use this vital knowledge to determine how the poet said it, by identifying and explaining the expressive techniques that the poet used. This is the second stage of poetry analysis.

To conduct the second stage effectively, you will need to use the appropriate terminology, for example, by referring to stanzas not paragraphs. If you are not familiar with this language, you may need to borrow or purchase a textbook that outlines and explains it so you know what to look for and how to describe it. This second stage of the analysis has two components. It involves identifying various expressive techniques that can be used in any form of writing but are particularly important in poetry (such as alliteration, assonance, metaphor, irony, etc.) and explaining how they convey the meaning of the poem. It also involves commenting on the form of the poem, noting how the rhyme and the rhythm complement the meaning, these qualities being determined by patterns in the choice of words and the punctuation. This task is easier than many students assume. You just describe the structure using the appropriate terminology and then link it to the meaning of the poem. For example:

> The poem consisted of one long stanza of twelve lines, with many lines being of different lengths. This free verse structure gave the poet the liberty to use punctuation to emphasise those elements of his message that he felt were more important and worthy of greater reader attention.

If you find published analyses of precisely the poem you are studying, avail yourself of this assistance and make your task easier. However, a word of warning, poetry analysis is extremely difficult, so be wary about the possibility that some interpretations may be problematic. To benefit from the opinions of others, you need to use their work critically.

Another word of warning, because poetry analysis is so difficult there is a chance that the poem may be beyond the capacity of your teacher to comprehend. Although many teachers advocate poetry as if it is good for you, like eating green vegetables, they can have great difficulty understanding it themselves. They can misunderstand it but not realise that they have done so. This means that those students who interpreted the poem correctly risk being penalised because their answer differs from the teacher's interpretation. If you seek high grades, it is crucial to pay close attention to the teacher's comments in class. If the teacher's interpretation differs, reflect the teacher's understanding of the poem in your answer even if you suspect that it is wrong. Poetry analysis is often an occasion when students are rewarded for reflecting the teacher's incorrect understanding rather than for presenting a correct interpretation. On the other hand, if the poetry analysis is part of an exam that is assessed externally, it will pay to ignore the teacher's incorrect analysis in favour of your own correct interpretation, thereby avoiding the cruel surprise that awaits those students who relied on the teacher's faulty understanding.

Literature reviews

Tertiary students may be asked to write a literature review, which is different to literature analysis although it involves using skills involved in literature analysis. A literature review can be an essay in its own right or form part of a major essay, like an Honours, Masters or Doctoral thesis. A literature review is an essay that reviews or assesses how helpful the existing relevant literature may be towards answering a question. This distinguishes it from a standard essay that uses various sources (literature) to actually answer a question on a topic. The literature review categorises this literature then assesses its usefulness in terms of achieving a particular purpose. In a thesis, it is used to justify the research undertaken for the thesis. It acknowledges the strengths, accomplishments, and turning points in the literature but more importantly, it points out the gaps, problem areas, or complexities that require attention and justifies the contribution to the field that the student wishes to make through their thesis.

Writing a literature review can be very demanding because of the volume of reading that can be involved with some topics. It requires students to assemble the relevant literature and organise it chronologically, then analyse and categorise the contribution made by each text, before writing the review, or, more precisely, the overview. The student's task is made much easier by drawing on existing literature reviews written by others, which may be found in the introductory chapters of some books, in academic articles devoted to reviewing the literature, or in theses on the same subject in your university library, this being because a literature review is a compulsory requirement for a thesis. Keep in mind that these other reviews were written, in part, to make the efforts of subsequent scholars, like yourself, easier, so if you build on their foundation, you are only doing what they hoped others would do. However, you need to be careful to use these reviews as guides rather than rely on them completely, since they were probably written with a different purpose in mind than your own. Despite the contribution of these pathfinders, you will still have do a substantial amount of your own surveying of the literature.

Another word of caution, examiners tend to be harsh on students who adopt a tone that they deem inappropriate. Traditionally, students are expected to be respectful regarding the work of significant scholars in the field, moderate in their criticism of the contributions of other scholars and modest in their justification of their own research efforts. A breech of this protocol can result in a severe penalty, which would be additionally disappointing considering the amount of work required to write a literature review. Fortunately, this danger is easily avoided through a judicious choice of language.

Research reports

Students working in the sciences or social sciences may have to write a research report. It is the format used for presenting the findings of original primary research. If you know how to write an essay, a research report is relatively straightforward. It is very similar to the essay in that it includes most of the components of an essay and mounts an argument. However, it follows a marginally different formal structure, with each component of the report being identified by subheadings, such as the following:

Introduction (which includes the hypothesis), Methods, Results, Discussion, Conclusion, and Appendices. However, although there is a standard formula for presenting research reports, various university departments may have their own idiosyncratic preferences, which are usually strictly enforced, so it is essential to find out what they are and follow them closely.

The requirements of the research report are governed by an appreciation of the scientific method of gathering and testing knowledge through systematic observation and experiment. The research report presents information that should allow an examiner to make a judgement about the validity of the student's research findings even though the examiner may not have direct access to all the student's data. The material should also be seen to potentially enable another researcher to test the student's hypothesis by repeating the procedure to, as near as possible, replicate the result. Consequently, it is important for students to be credible in their argument, to only claim precisely what the evidence suggests and no more, in order to offer another modest addition to the store of knowledge in that field.

The introduction to a research report does much of what is done in the introduction to an essay. It explains your concerns that led you to the topic. It then it clearly defines the topic and your approach to it, as well as the key terms and theoretical concepts, to eliminate any ambiguity in the way that your project can be understood. The research report then clearly states your hypothesis that you sought to test, to confirm (in full or in part) or deny via your research. Like the contention in an essay, the hypothesis is the focal point of the research report because virtually everything in the report relates to it. Next, the research report discusses the methods used, with the intention of justifying them as a viable way to test the hypothesis by explaining their strengths while acknowledging their limitations.

The two following sections headed Results and Discussion correspond to the body of an essay. The results section presents data that the research discovered, while the discussion section explores the implications of the data for the hypothesis. This is where students are expected to show intellectual flair as they carefully reflect on the findings to determine precisely what can be learnt from the project, including an appreciation of any unintended consequences and the effectiveness of the method.

Finally, just like in an essay, the conclusion sums up the argument. If the hypothesis is confirmed, then it will be presented as a contribution to knowledge. If it is confirmed only in part or denied, then the conclusion will reflect these findings. Added to the end of the research report are appendices that may include, for example, a copy of the questionnaire that was used to conduct a survey, tables of raw data, or anything else that would allow the examiner to replicate the research or scrutinise the methods used. To be an effective piece of writing, the research report should have a quality of professional competence and completeness regarding its formal requirements. It should also exhibit qualities of thoroughness, astuteness, precision and proportion in regards to its examination and assessment of the findings.

Essays for (non-academic) vocational courses

While research reports are strictly formal in their structure and presentation, essays for non-academic vocational courses, such as hotel management, are far less concerned with the technical requirements of scholarship. By contrast, while good scholarship may be appreciated, the key to doing well in these essays is to demonstrate that you can apply the theories and procedures that you have been taught to solve practical problems and produce tangibly beneficial outcomes. The educators who conduct these courses are usually drawn from the relevant industries so, while they may be reasonably well read in their subject, their points of reference for assessing students' work also includes firsthand experience. Consequently, they usually value clarity and common sense in expression and reasoning, qualities that students submitting essays in these courses need to demonstrate.

Problem-solving exercises

In addition to essays, problem-solving exercises in various forms turn up in a wide range of subjects, especially in mathematics, the sciences, accounting, or in branches of philosophy like logic. This involves learning formulas or theories and applying them to solve problems. Problem-solving exercises can be demanding. The acquisition of the knowledge of these formulas or theories is only the first step rather than the final objective of study. What matters, is how this knowledge is used to perform a range of exercises. The key to success is to increase your expertise, and this involves deepening your knowledge of the formulas or theories and then practising their application in every conceivable circumstance. Rather than memorising a formula or theory without fully understanding it, students become better equipped to apply it effectively if they find out about the origins of the formula or theory, why it takes the form it does, and what its purposes are. The better you understand a formula or theory, the better you become at applying it competently. The next stage is to practise, beginning with easier exercises and progressing to the more demanding problems. It can help to have the necessary formulas or theories handy as you work, so you can refer to them whenever you need reminding. Through practice, this knowledge will become second nature to you. As you test the formulas with many and varied applications, eventually you will achieve such a degree of competence that further practice seems unnecessary. At this point, you are primed for success in any assignment, test or exam.

When you study the formulas or theories and practise their application, it is important to work at a pace at which you feel comfortable. Allow yourself the time it takes you to understand something. Be prepared to encounter obstacles on your path to expertise. Sometimes it will help if you put a troublesome problem aside and approach it the next day with a fresh mind. You should also be careful to avoid practising your mistakes. If an approach is not producing the desired result, you probably need to deepen your understanding before you can resume practising productively. It may help to have some clever friends, considerate educators or even an expert private tutor on hand to resolve what is hindering your progress. Be aware that the very satisfying feeling associated with having achieved expertise usually creeps up on you gradually. It will be evident when you feel that you can handle any problem thrown at you, and when you believe you can teach the formulas or theories profitably to others.

Public speaking: From competence to mastery

On several occasions during your secondary and tertiary education, you will be asked to do some public speaking, which is also known as oratory or as making an oral presentation. Curiously, even though students are graded on these exercises, they are rarely if ever taught the art of public speaking. Students are usually just thrown into the deep end and expected to swim. This is often because even though most teachers regularly speak in front of classes, they know very little about oratory. Many teachers merely learn to cope with public speaking through experience, muddling through rather than excelling at it. Although some teachers cope very well, often they do not fully understand what is involved in their success. They just do it. Teachers may be able to give their classes some pointers on how to cope, but they are usually not able to teach oratory perceptively. Ironically, the teachers are of course the very people who will be assessing the students' efforts. Although, they may have been provided with official criteria to guide their assessment, to a significant degree most of them are simply 'winging it', responding to the speaker's performance like anyone else in the audience. Consequently, in regards to public speaking, it makes sense to view most teachers as somewhat like amateur art critics; they may not know much about art but they know what they like. Most people appreciate good public speaking, and the teachers who are assessing you are no different. This means that if you speak well, you will usually be well rewarded with high grades.

I was not taught the art of oratory at school or university either, but the skill fascinated me, so I carefully scrutinised the performances of some of history's great orators to determine the relationship between these speakers and their audiences and what they were doing that persuaded and moved their audiences. I also scrutinised ineffective speakers, and studied what they were doing incorrectly so it could be avoided. From this reflection and analysis, as well as from refining this understanding through practice, I distilled and refined several guiding principles that I have used to help many students excel, including those who initially regarded public speaking as their greatest challenge.

Our goal of enabling you to learn the art of public speaking will be helped if you recognise that you may already be closer to being an effective public speaker than you thought. You have probably already spoken effectively on many occasions, such as when telling family members some interesting news or when putting forward your point of view in a discussion with friends. On these occasions with small familiar audiences, you spoke coherently, expressively, confidently and persuasively. Public speaking is the same but it takes place in a different environment. If you can already speak persuasively to an audience of one or a few people, you already have the capacity to be an effective public speaker with larger audiences. This knowledge should make you more relaxed and confident about it, which is our first step towards doing it well. To progress further, we need to deepen our understanding of what is involved.

You may also be reassured to know that talks are composed in a similar fashion to essays, so most of what we learnt about effective writing regarding structure, style, and language is relevant, indeed essential, to public speaking. We will build upon this wisdom, modifying and adding to it. Where talks principally differ from essays is that they have an additional expressive dimension, the delivery or performance. I encourage you to see the performance as an opportunity because it gives you greater control over how your words are interpreted and the chance to infuse much more emotional force or meaning to the content of your material.

The key to effective public speaking is rapport. As we have previously noted, rapport refers to feelings of like-mindedness, affinity, or mutual connectedness. Before you can establish this rapport between yourself as the speaker and your audience, you will need to know two things – your audience and yourself. People like like-minded people, those with whom they share things in common. If you demonstrate that you share significant likes and dislikes with your audience, which consists of your teacher (who is your examiner) and the other students in the class, then you have increased the likelihood that they will appreciate you and your talk. It will help significantly if you choose subject matter that is in tune with the biases of your audience, so you are seen to reinforce their beliefs and values. Alternatively, if you are attempting to take the audience in a different direction or introduce them to new material, you will need to choose a perspective or approach to the subject matter that the audience can relate to as like their own. When attempting to appeal to potentially diverse audience segments, such as the teacher and the students, you may seek to find common ground that simultaneously appeals to both segments. On the other hand, if this is not possible, choose to appeal to the most important element, who is in this case the teacher, although there is a chance that a positive reaction from the larger audience segment, the students, may be infectious. Importantly, the establishment of rapport is achieved through more than the content of the talk, it is also achieved through the manner of your presentation, the audible tone of your language and the way you look at and physically present yourself to the audience. The audience needs to be able to relate to the speaker's attitude and physical presence.

When seeking to establish rapport and make a positive impression on the audience, an effective public speaker also has to have a sense of their own capabilities and limitations. You should capitalise on your capabilities and compensate for or bypass your limitations. If you lack experience as a public speaker, you may seek the reassurance of a scripted performance or seek to build your confidence by becoming an expert on your subject. If you speak in broken English because English is your second language, you may seek to infuse your performance with such infectious enthusiasm for your subject that your broken English is regarded as inconsequential or charming.

If you know your capabilities and limitations, you can choose the level at which you can perform. The art of public speaking can be conducted at either of three skill levels, the basic, intermediate, or advanced. Talks conducted at each of these levels can be very effective, so success is not dependent on progressing to the advanced level. The basic or intermediate skill levels are sufficient to produce high grades in talks at school and university, so either of these may be sufficient for most students. Meanwhile the advanced level is for those students who want to take the art of public speaking to an even greater degree of control and accomplishment. After outlining what is involved at working at each level, I shall share with you the principles that will make your talks more effective at any level and enable you to progress as far as you wish to go with this form of expression.

The basic skill level involves performing from a written speech that serves as a script, which may be read from note paper or hand cards, usually with the key words, headings, or phrases highlighted to assist the performance. The speaker reads, while taking the opportunity to look up at the audience as often as possible to maintain or enhance some sense of connection or rapport. Although the quality of the delivery may vary marginally from rehearsal to performance, the content remains the same. This approach suits those students who are less experienced and who want the reassurance of working from a carefully prepared written document. The delivery involved with this approach can be very effective, although the degree of rapport with the audience is compromised due to the reliance on notes. On the other hand, if the language is well chosen, its quality may compensate somewhat for the reliance on notes.

The intermediate skill level involves speaking from a list of reminder notes. The speaker may draft a speech, which is then reduced to a list of reminder notes consisting of headings or key phrases. The speaker talks directly to the audience except when it is necessary to look down at the notes, from time to time, to be reminded of what to discuss next. With this approach, some of the accuracy is lost in terms of the verbatim communication of prepared dialogue, but a much more profound connection or rapport with the audience can be achieved through the performance. Consequently, this approach can generate a greater impact than talks delivered at the basic level. While most students are content to work at the basic level where they feel more secure, others aspire to reach the intermediate level, which can better appeal to those examiners who prefer this form of presentation to scripted performances. Although, the basic and intermediate skill levels are both suitable for delivering high grades in classroom presentations, public speaking can be taken to a considerably more advanced level, which you can observe being practised by politicians and entertainers as well as by talented lecturers. While it is not necessary to speak at this advanced level to do well in classroom presentations, by learning some of the principles involved in attaining and performing at this level you will be able to perform better at any level.

The advanced skill level relies on fewer sources of support and reassurance because the speaker is experienced and confident enough to feel that they are no longer necessary. Although, the speech may have originally been fully drafted, to make the speaker conversant with the material, it was subsequently reduced to a sequence of key points and phrases that are learnt. Alternatively, an experienced confident speaker may skip drafting a complete script, instead producing a coherent outline that includes several scripted insightful comments or revealing anecdotes or witty remarks. Following this, the talk is virtually put together live. The speakers who operate at this advanced level of skill can speak to the audience without notes, which usually impresses audiences. Consequently, the delivery can have a quality of immediacy, because the speaker can tune into the audience more profoundly, to feed off and perhaps adjust the performance to suit the audience's mood. The most able speakers can then employ sophisticated techniques to change its mood. Because the speaker can exercise an astute flexibility to adapt to different audiences and circumstances, repeated performances of the same speech may differ noticeably in terms of their tone and content. With this approach to delivery, some of the content originally intended for use may be inadvertently overlooked. However, because the speaker is effectively tuned into the audience, rapport is maximised, so the missing material often hardly matters. Public speaking conducted at this level is usually the most effective, although similar very positive responses can be achieved by talks conducted at the intermediate level.

We have previously noted that talks are composed in virtually the same fashion as essays. We have also previously noted that clarity and simplicity are important qualities for writing effectively. In public speaking, they are crucial. When composing the content of your talk, keep the story simple. Focus on the major themes and points, and skip most of the less important material. Talks can carry far less complexity than written texts. While readers can afford to pause and reflect on difficult material until it is understood, listeners prefer to keep pace with the speaker. In addition, avoid using long lists of names, or presenting too much detail or too much data. While fascinating when read to oneself, it can be tedious when communicated verbally. Keep the material simple. Mention only the essential characters or details and generalise about the rest. Unlike when reading silently to themselves, listeners find it inconvenient to digest detailed information. Above all, you must keep the story flowing. This means the structure of the talk makes a crucial contribution to its effectiveness.

Just as with a written essay, you need to organise your argument into a coherent logical structure. Present an argument or story that flows in a logical manner. Remember our principle for understanding the nature of art: Works of art are a series of ideas presented in a sequence that is ultimately intended to produce an emotional response. With this in mind, you may play around with the sequence of ideas to create the desired effects in the audience, perhaps to create surprise or suspense or fascination. In addition, if the material is logically structured, you will be more comfortable in delivering it because its sequence is more conducive to being reduced to a list of reminder points and consequently more likely to be remembered. As a result, you may even be able to deliver it without having to resort to reading a script or looking at your reminder notes.

Another means to progress from relying on a written speech to speaking off the cuff, is to shift the focus of your preparation from aiming to deliver precise lines of dialogue to communicating ideas. It is easier to remember ideas, especially if they are organised in a logical sequence. Stories have a beginning, middle and end, and once the telling has commenced, they usually have a logic that carries the speaker through to the conclusion. Even if you forget the exact lines of dialogue that you originally conceived, you will often come up with similar lines during the performance that are just as effective. Be prepared to think on your feet and to accept that the talk may take a slightly different path than originally planned. Although there may be less precision in your dialogue, there will be more spontaneity and conviction in your presentation. Like riding a bicycle for the first time, you may be shaky at your first attempt at speaking publicly without a script, but your confidence will grow with experience.

Those seeking to perform at the intermediate or advanced levels, also need to appreciate that the preparation for a talk is much like that for an exam, where the material is initially studied in a coherent fashion, then expressed according to the circumstances that present themselves at the moment that the talk is delivered. This is not unlike the way that exam responses fashion knowledge to conform to suit previously unseen questions. There is a degree of spontaneity involved in delivering a talk in this fashion, as the tone of the delivery and the contents are adapted to suit the circumstances.

The qualities of clarity and simplicity that are crucial to the structure of the talk are also crucial to the choice of effective language. An extensive tract of writing in scholarly English can be quite acceptable when read silently to oneself, but when read aloud to an audience it can sometimes be difficult to follow. While most teachers expect to hear students use scholarly English in their talks, there needs to be some modifications to this language to maximise its effectiveness when spoken. Consequently, some of the conventions of scholarly English need to be adjusted.

In public speaking the language needs to be simpler and clearer than in written speech because if the listeners are forced to pause and reflect on the meaning of a word they can fall behind, dropping out of the flow of the talk. If they lose their connection to the speaker, they may become lost from the audience. If this happens to too many people, the audience becomes alienated. Consequently, it is important to avoid big obscure words. Curiously, while many teachers are generally impressed by big words and frown upon the use of simple words, some compromise needs to be found so that the vocabulary is impressive but accessible. Similarly, avoid using jargon, abbreviations, acronyms or anything else that entails a risk of being misunderstood. Instead, spell things out clearly (for example, say weapons of mass destruction rather than WMDs) so that the audience can easily follow everything that is said.

In addition, it can add flavour to a talk if it is occasionally spiced with a dash of expressive colloquial language or slang at a key moment, or sweetened by some conversational English, even though these elements would usually be frowned upon in written essays. In a talk, they can make the material more expressive, enjoyable and accessible, but be careful, and make sure that your audience is comfortable with these elements. If they work, use them, if they do not, omit them. Furthermore, various attention grabbing techniques, such as humour, unusual anecdotes, or curious illustrations are often regarded as superfluous in scholarly writing, but in talks they are valuable means to connect and reconnect to an audience as well as to entertain them. Ideally, you should also put into practice what we have learnt about how language is understood emotionally. Think of the emotional effects that you want to generate in the audience and choose language that complements that objective. Be aware of the principle behind the way that the expressions 'I will not disappoint you' and 'I will help you succeed' say almost the same thing at one level but at another emotional level they create different effects in the audience. In public speaking, an appreciation of the emotional effects of language can be a vital ingredient in producing the greatest emotional responses from the audience.

To gain confidence for your delivery, make sure you know your subject well. The reassuring aura of relaxed authority that comes with this knowledge will also encourage the audience to have confidence in the speaker. In addition, you should prepare sufficiently so you can regard yourself positively as an interesting person with something interesting to say. Even though an awareness of what can go wrong is helpful during the preparation of a talk because it makes you aware of contingencies that you may need to address, it is important to dismiss any negative thoughts before the performance. Do what is required to deal with any potential problems beforehand, so you can maintain a positive internal dialogue before the event. This positive attitude about yourself and the task should be reinforced by focusing on what you have achieved in composing the talk and what you seek to achieve in delivering it. To maintain this positive disposition, you may also choose to recall previous events when everything went right for you, so you can tune into those positive feelings and allow them to carry you through the upcoming event. Your attitude is crucial in public speaking. A positive attitude lays the foundation for victory before the battle is fought.

To create the appropriate inflections in your voice, rather than those false, forced, artificial theatrical inflections that can annoy audiences, simply say the words as if you mean them, then the inflections will be there naturally, resonating with sincerity just as they do when you converse with family or friends. Some words will be sad or dramatic or uplifting or light-hearted, and if you say the words as if you mean them, then your voice will reflect the appropriate feelings to make the speech more engaging. This point about effective delivery is deceptively simple, so do not underestimate it. Some students are not used to reading aloud in this fashion, having fallen into a bad habit of reading in a monotone. Rehearsals should focus on saying the words as if you mean them, thereby developing this sincerity of feeling that can add so much power to the delivery of the talk. In addition, it is important to speak slowly, at a pace that allows the words to resonate the richness of their meanings. This will allow you to give an audible emphasis to the key words or to pause to heighten their impact. If you speak slowly, you will be communicating more clearly and expressively. Keep practising your material until you are speaking with sincere feeling in your voice. Remember to say it as if you mean it. This simple principle has been one of the most effective that my students have employed to revolutionise their performances to succeed in a task that they formerly found challenging.

The confidence that stems from your knowledge of your subject, and the reassurance achieved by practising the dialogue, will often translate into a positive physical demeanor and expressive gestures that are both natural and appropriate. If you are genuinely interested in your material and you care about communicating it to your audience, your physical appearance should naturally reinforce your message and work in your favour, just as it does when you are talking informally to family or friends. Rather than seeking to artificially infuse expressive gestures into your performance, let them happen naturally. The audience in a classroom is close enough to see and appreciate subtlety. Only speakers who have to address huge auditoriums need to exaggerate their gestures to make an impression on the audience members who are too distant to notice anything less dramatic.

When delivering your talk to the audience, no matter how large, it can be more effective if you pretend you are speaking to one person rather than a group. This is a more familiar experience and it can make a speaker feel more relaxed. Moreover, it can also improve the performance, by generating a quality of intimacy between the speaker and the audience that is conducive to generating rapport. An effective public speaker can also be seen to 'work the room', looking at one section of the audience during one part of the speech and then at another section for another part. If you are looking in the direction of a particular section of the audience, it makes that part of the speech being expressed seem special or memorable to them. You may seek to use this effect to make a stronger impression on certain sections of the audience when you feel it is appropriate to do so.

While the purpose of art, including public speaking, is to generate an emotional response in the audience, you should never directly try to move them emotionally. Instead, you move them indirectly. Once you have established a connection, as your emotions change then those of your audience should change with you. This is the power that great orators have, their secret. It is the orator's ability to generate feelings in themselves that in turn generate them in their audiences that makes for the most effective speeches. These feelings need not be as dramatic as profound sadness or elation. Instead, they might be something like the infectious enthusiasm or a sense of fascination that the speaker brings to the subject, which are, of course, the emotional responses best suited to most classroom presentations. People tend to remember the emotions that a speaker generated more so than the content of a speech. Try to recall a speech that you appreciated. You may have difficulty remembering any of the dialogue, but you can certainly remember the emotion that you felt while in the audience.

Remember that you can only move an audience to follow your emotional lead if you have initially established a connection. This can be achieved with an anecdote with which people can identify or via a witty remark that entertains them. You would have noticed that many speakers open their talks with a joke. They do this because they know it breaks the ice and establishes a positive mood. They may not fully realise this, but it is also a means to establish the essential connection between the speaker and the audience that lays the foundation for taking the audience on a more profoundly moving emotional journey. Humour is one means of achieving this. Stories that people can relate to in a substantial manner are also effective. An astute public speaker usually waits until he feels that a connection has been established and reinforced before he turns up the emotional heat. Once this has been achieved, he can take the audience virtually wherever he wants to go.

An advantage that comes from generating an emotional response within an audience is that it can become infectious. If you have ever found yourself laughing at an incident solely because everyone else in the room was laughing, then you have experienced the impact of crowd behaviour. If the majority of the crowd enthusiastically supports the speaker, then others in the crowd may be induced to follow. This phenomenon is well known, but its effects are sometimes overestimated, since we can all recall many occasions when we constituted a dissenting spirit within a crowd. But what is also known is that if many people experience the same emotion at the same time, it can be intensified, in a similar fashion to the way that it can be more satisfying to watch an entertaining film in the company of others rather than alone. Therefore, if you can make an impact on an audience, the emotional pay off can be substantial indeed.

At university, most of the public speaking that students are expected to perform involves presenting tutorial papers, which involves reading an essay to the tutorial group. The paper is later collected by the tutor or lecturer who was present and graded as an essay rather than as a talk, so it needs to be drafted as an essay rather than as a talk. This somewhat restricts what students can do with the material to make it more listener-friendly. Nevertheless, many essays can be drafted clearly and expressively so they read well silently and aloud. Moreover, when presenting the paper, students should apply the basic skills of reading expressively to create a positive impression during the tutorial. In addition, postgraduate students may be asked to conduct a work-in-progress seminar on their thesis. If you can conduct it using the intermediate or advanced public speaking skills, it will be more effective and work to your advantage in other ways, impressing those academics present that you have the lecturing skills to make a fine future academic, if that is your wish.

Course applications and interviews

While we are on the topic of speaking well to impress lecturers, some of you, at some stage in your education, may have to write an application and pass an interview to be selected into the tertiary course of your choice. Students often feel anxious about these tasks because so much is at stake and they are not sure what they have to do to succeed. It is to this important topic that we shall now turn. It may please you to know that success in these important tasks involves applying knowledge that we have already learnt.

If you want to apply successfully for a course, firstly you have to decide whether you merely want to cross this task off your 'to do' list or you want to really succeed in achieving your objective. If you really want to succeed, then you have to be prepared to do those extra things that will significantly increase your chances, these things being what most others find inconvenient to do. What I am about to share with you can dramatically shift the odds in your favour, from success being possible to being likely. What is involved is not difficult but it requires some diligent work. The key to a successful course application and interview is preparatory research. You need to find out what the selectors think they want, and determine what they actually want, then appear to provide both.

Most school students do not know what qualities the academics on course selection panels are looking for in prospective students. This is because most students assume that these academics want what school authorities find appealing, such as respect for the ethos and reputation of the school, and the capacity to fit in with that ethos and add positively to the reputation of the school by producing high grades or by showing proficiency in sporting or other co-curricular activities. The display of these qualities will help prospective students win admittance into the school of their choice, but universities are different. They are more pluralistic than schools. Most university faculties, in a practical sense, have little or nothing to do with the other faculties, so references to the reputation of the university as a whole or to co-curricular activities will not persuade the academics on the selection panel. Academics tend to see themselves as employed by their respective departments within their relevant faculties. The departments tend to operate as institutions unto themselves, and many academics are more interested in research than teaching. They prefer keen dedicated students with interests and capabilities suited precisely to the courses on offer, who will cause the department little fuss because they will flow through to graduate within the minimum period. They also value students who show the potential to eventually conduct postgraduate research, which can moderately enhance the prestige of the department by adding to its research output. Furthermore, they may also prefer students who seem like individuals who may be pleasant to have around the department. In addition to these factors, the applicant needs to appreciate that academics are sages, so they gain great personal satisfaction in knowing that their work is read and appreciated. While the other factors are important, this yearning for appreciation is their principal weakness and your surest key to success.

Begin your campaign by investigating the relevant university department by checking the university website or faculty handbook. Determine the subject areas covered by the available courses so you can argue that a particular course they offer is perfectly suited to your interests and needs. **The more that you resemble an experienced (first year) student rather than a naïve applicant, the more impressive you will be to the course selection panel.** You should look up the course reading guide and select a comprehensive or general textbook that is central to the course, then read it. It is fine to show enthusiasm and interest in the relevant subject areas. It is far more impressive to have demonstrated your enthusiasm by having already acquired some knowledge. You can do even better than this. You can use the course reading guide to familiarise yourself with some of the major books and academic journals in the field. Find them in the university library and leaf through them so you have an idea what they are like. By doing this, you are becoming familiar with the world of your prospective educators. The more familiar you seem to be with this world, the more likely they will be to welcome you into it as a student with potential. With this knowledge, you would have demonstrated to them that you would probably do well at the course and probably acquire the ability to continue on to postgraduate research.

It also helps to show a clear direction of interest, which is a line of academic inquiry that you wish to pursue. This needs to correspond with the expertise of the available lecturers. Consequently, the selectors will believe that you are ideal for their course and they are ideally positioned to help you. In addition, despite this sense of purpose, you must also show an open-minded curiosity to learn in ways that you had not originally anticipated. This gives members of the selection panel the opportunity to believe that they can mould you into a scholar after their own image. It also helps to project likeable qualities, so you seem like a person whom they would like to have around the department. The members of the selection panel are understandably interested in maintaining a workplace where they feel relaxed and comfortable. Ensure that you give the impression that you would contribute positively to this environment.

Most importantly, you should investigate the academics who teach the course by looking them up in the university library, then familiarising yourself with their publications. You do not have to become an expert on their writings, just familiar enough to praise their work intelligently. This is so you can argue that, for example, you do not simply want to study architecture but rather study architecture under these particular lecturers whose writings you admire. Academics find this approach virtually irresistible. There is only one risk. Academics tend to be competitive and rivalrous. You need to avoid the chance that your admiration for one academic may disappoint an envious rival. There are two ways to steer clear of this. You can spread your admiration widely.

Alternatively, you can contact the department to find out who is on the selection panel so you can ensure that you praise the work of precisely the academic to whom you are speaking at the interview. Bull's eye! As you talk, you can gain encouragement by watching an irrepressible smile of satisfaction appear in the face of the selector.

The better prepared that you are, the more confident you will be in drafting your application letter and during the interview. If you can show yourself to be more knowledgeable and capable than most of the competing candidates, you need not be concerned about revealing a few signs of naiveté or immaturity or wide-eyed enthusiasm. These qualities are expected in young hopefuls, and when combined with some relevant knowledge and demonstrated initiative, they are endearing. The students of mine who have used these powerful techniques have been extremely successful in achieving their objectives. It is well worth the extra effort.

Job applications and interviews

By the way, the skills that you can apply to succeed at course applications and interviews are the same that will enable you to succeed at job hunting. They can help you to get the jobs you need to support yourself through university and to later achieve employment in the career of your choice after graduation. When applying for a position of employment, preparatory research is essential. Try to think of the job from the perspective of the employer, in terms of what they hope to gain rather than what you hope to gain. Find out the aims of the business, the qualities they are looking for in the person to fill the available position, and determine the values and culture of the organisation. This is so you can word your application so you appear to be able to contribute to the achievement of the businesses' goals, to have all the qualities that they are seeking, and to fit in perfectly with the values and culture of the organisation.

Job ads tell you very little, so you will need to contact the organisation to find out more. It is essential that you overcome any shyness and make contact with someone in the organisation. You may initially quiz the receptionist for clues, before being put through to the personnel officer or the manager to ask them directly about the organisation and what they are looking for in an employee. This may sound precocious. That is because it is, because precociousness is what is necessary. More than enabling you to find out the crucial information to enable you to tailor your application to maximise its appeal, it puts you ahead of the pack and gets you noticed. You would have established yourself as a real flesh and blood person by becoming a voice on the telephone rather than first coming to their attention as a piece of paper in the form of a written application, something that can more easily be dismissed. In making contact, you have also demonstrated your genuine interest by taking the initiative to meet them. In addition, you may also have recruited an advocate within the organisation. If you have impressed the secretary, or someone else in the organisation who can have a friendly informal word to the employer on your behalf, it can greatly enhance your prospects.

With the necessary information at your disposal, you can construct your written application and interview performance to press all the right psychological buttons. For your interview, dress in a smarter neater version of what you would wear to do the job, so it is easy for them to picture you in that role. That means you would wear a suit to an interview for a clerical position but not to become a labourer. You should also dress to conform to the workplace culture of the organisation. Some employers prefer a more casually dressed workforce than others do, and would be looking for someone who looked as if they would fit in to this office culture. You should be aware that during the process of filling the vacancy, the employer is continually quietly making calculations as to whether the candidate meets their requirements. **With job applications and interviews, the trick is to give the employers the information that leads their calculations in the direction that you want them to take. To win, you do not have to be the best applicant, only a successful one. They are not necessarily the same.**

CHAPTER 4

CLOSING THOUGHTS

Together, we have learnt a great deal. We have learnt practical skills on how to organise the resources you will need to achieve consistent success in the education system, along with budgeting and how to find the jobs to support yourself through this period of scholastic toil and sacrifice, skills that you can later use to enter the careers that for many students constitute their ultimate objective. In addition, we learnt how to write effective excuse or permission letters. These skills deal with dimensions of the overall study experience that can sometimes be decisive yet are often overlooked by students.

We also have learnt much about how to achieve high results through merit, by looking in detail at the art of learning through reading and note-taking. In addition, we looked closely at the art of research, essay writing and public speaking, the objective being to enable you to achieve mastery over these key dimensions of the educational experience. This book is intended to enable you to reskill from scratch, allowing you to rebuild, revitalise or replace your previous study skills with new ones that can take you farther, skills that you can profitably use to succeed in the education system and elsewhere, throughout your life.

However, although merit is very important, and valuable for its own sake, it is no guarantee of consistent success in the education system unless it is combined with a profound understanding of the realities regarding assessment and what is going on in the minds of examiners during this process. Consequently, we also learnt a revolutionary new approach that I describe as the Method, a psychological approach that shows you how to make the most of valuable information that is all around you, which is often overlooked, that can tip the power balance decisively in your favour.

To this end, we learnt how you can cultivate the kinds of student personas that educators prefer to reward and how to create psychological profiles of your examiners to ensure that everything you put into your work to be assessed will pay a dividend in grades.

Through this volume, you have already learnt much that can make a significant positive difference to your education. However, in Volume 2 we will deepen your knowledge of the assessment process even further to learn, among other things, how to turn a prejudicial or hostile teacher into an agent of your success. In addition, we will also look at exams and learn how to make them an easier option. Finally, we will look at the process of changing yourself from the inside, to adopt the attitudes and qualities that make success more likely.

Although these volumes provide many practical skills, above all they are about appreciating the transformative power of ideas. Like most students, you would have previously done the best you could with what you knew at the time. Now that you know much more, you can do much better. This book has something to help everyone who is seeking to do well in the education system. However, those of you who will get the most out of this book are those who love ideas.

An idea can positively transform a person's life. An idea can turn the barriers that once intolerably held you back into mere hurdles that you leap over in your race to success. An idea can set you free. Winning ideas are more than comprehended – these are ideas that you feel. With ideas like these, you feel rearmed and ready for renewed struggle. The purpose of this book is to arm you with an idea of this kind: **Success in the education system primarily depends on how effectively you deal with people in authority over you.** This is the idea at the foundation of everything that I have taught you. It is an idea that makes the formerly incoherent suddenly coherent, thereby making the possible, probable. Enjoy using it.

www.ingramcontent.com/pod-product-compliance
Lightning Source LLC
Chambersburg PA
CBHW052044300426
44117CB00012B/1972